G000047782

Invoking Angels

RABBI DAVID A. COOPER

INVOKING ANGELS

FOR BLESSINGS, PROTECTION, AND HEALING

SOUNDS TRUE

Sounds True, Inc.
Boulder CO 80306

© 2006 Rabbi David A. Cooper ℗ Sounds True

SOUNDS TRUE is a trademark of Sounds True, Inc.
All rights reserved. No part of this book or CD may be used or reproduced
in any manner without written permission from the author and publisher.

10 9 8 7 6 5 4 3 2

Published 2006
Printed in Korea
David A. Cooper:
        Invoking Angels

ISBN 978-1-59179-518-6

Library of Congress Control Number 2006928853

TABLE OF CONTENTS

Preface   ix

Introduction   1

Part One   8
A Mystical Understanding of Angels

Part Two   26
Angels in the Bible

Part Three   36
The Main Archangels

Part Four   56
The Supreme Angels

Part Five   70
The Fallen Angels

Acknowledgments   85

About the Author   89

Preface

MY FIRST CONTACT with God and angels occurred when I was ten years old. I lived on the north side of Chicago and was experiencing my very first infatuation. She lived across the street, and her name was Carole. A ten-year-old's "love" can be all-consuming. I remember clearly one day absolutely needing to tell her something. To my dismay, she was not home, and I could not find her anywhere. So I made one of those impulsive moves that can somehow affect us for the rest of our lives. I called out to the great, mysterious unknown and made my bargain: "If there really is a God, I promise I will believe in you forever if you help me find Carole right away!"

Now, over fifty years have passed since that moment, and it still rings clear in my mind. It so happened that only a few minutes after my rash (but heartfelt) commitment, a friend (angel) walked up to me and said, for no apparent reason, "David, I just saw Carole at …" I was dumbstruck! This was a terrific lesson for me, but at that point getting to Carole was more important than enlightenment. So I did not stop to ponder my awe, but ran instead to meet my beloved. Nonetheless, although this promise to believe in God forever was born in an impulsive childhood moment, it continues to sit in my heart to this day. I must say, however, that my perspective of the meaning of God and the purpose of angels has changed dramatically over the years in a way that has turned out to influence profoundly the direction of my life and the work that I do.

More than thirty years had passed after that initial experience when my wife, Shoshana, and I moved to the Old City of Jerusalem. It was in the mid-eighties, and we were on a serious spiritual quest. While living and studying in the Old City for many years, we frequently experienced a curious event that most residents there take for granted. Almost every time we would discuss the need to meet someone or to invite someone to a meal, that person would appear. Strangely and almost miraculously, within hours, the phone would ring, or we would run into that person on the street. This happened so frequently that any time someone's name came up in conversation, we simply assumed that a meeting with this person was imminent.

We all experience synchronistic events like these throughout our lives. We can approach this unique phenomenon with scientific curiosity, but we are not likely to get far. Events like these do not easily lend themselves to evaluation, repetition, or measurement—each of which is a necessary component of the scientific method. Yet, we know them when they happen because in those moments something deep inside of us is comforted in a tender way; we experience an inexpressible sense of satisfaction, of feeling connected with a mysterious something that holds the world together.

People who live in Jerusalem say that this synchrony happens more often there because the city has a mysterious *kedusha*, a word that means "sanctification" or "holiness." I came to realize, however, that it seemed to happen more often in Jerusalem because we who lived there were far more aware of and prepared for mystical experiences to arise. We were more aware because we immersed ourselves in biblical studies many hours every day, and we discussed written and oral religious traditions on a regular basis.

We all have had the experience of learning a new word and then suddenly hearing the word everywhere. We learn a new skill, such as painting, and then we start seeing colors through new eyes. We learn to play a musical instrument, and from that time forward we hear all music with new ears. The same phenomenon occurs when we engage deeply in certain types of studies. In the Jewish world, the study is of the Torah and all its commentaries. Immersed in these studies, one begins to see the world in a different light, a world filled with new mysteries. Included in those mysteries are realms beyond our ordinary reality, filled with supernatural energies. They are not "real" in the ordinary sense that we can measure them to meet scientific criteria, but they are real on some other level. They speak to us, guide us, protect us, caution us; they are voices and visions that appear clearly in the mind's eye.

There are many names and descriptions of supernal characters that show up in spiritual literature. There are thousands of them that fit into many different categories. One of the most popular categories is the realm of angels. A wide variety of angels are described in Christianity and Islam, as well as in Judaism. Moreover, they are not limited to Western tradition. There are many angels described in Tibetan Buddhism and Hinduism. Indeed, angels can be found in a wide variety of traditions.

This book is not designed to be a dictionary of all the different angelic characters that exist in a multitude of traditions, but rather to be a guide to introduce to the reader ways to invoke and work with specific characteristics that are connected with well-known angels. We will therefore discuss only a select number of angels that have been described extensively in the literature of Western tradition. In this process of exploring qualities associated with certain angels, we discover new possibilities of manifesting new capabilities within ourselves.

You should know that I have considerable skepticism when it comes to fanciful ideals about invisible beings who affect our lives. Anyone who has read my book *God Is a Verb* knows that I do not subscribe to the idea that God is a father figure who runs the creation, but is rather a process that is continuously in motion.

In the same spirit, my approach to angels does not delve into realms populated by critters with wings and halos. I have instead a deeper and much more subtle relationship with angels. As you will discover, I have an ongoing interaction with angels that evokes certain characteristics in a way that continuously informs my life. Evoking these characteristics is an empowering process. It can lead to greater strength in helping ourselves or others when working with difficult situations. This is not a skill that is unique to selected individuals; it is something that all human beings can access and develop if they wish.

The popular characterization of angels in Western tradition is that they are hidden beings that sometimes reveal themselves for various purposes. We have seen them in movies and on television; we read about them in the Torah, the New Testament, and the Qur'an; and we often talk about them when special things happen to us. When we read about or see angels like this, they are often mistaken for people; but they usually have magical powers, the ability to see one's past and future, and they appear and disappear at will. There are many books written about supernatural angels like these.

While the book you are now reading describes in some sections this more traditional perspective on angels, the emphasis is on how we can empower ourselves by invoking energies associated with specific angels. Doing so allows us to open up new possibilities for bringing blessings, protection, and healing to ourselves and others.

Each of the traditional archangels, for example, has unique attributes associated with it. Through the use of imagination and visualization, we can develop a psychospiritual relationship that brings these characteristics alive within us. In this way, we are able to access our own hidden strengths that we often do not realize we have. The process is similar to the discovery made by athletes who are able to improve their performances by visualizing success as they push themselves beyond their best efforts. In the same way, we can call in angelic images to help give us strength in dealing with any number of situations.

In addition, by understanding the nature of some of the truly extraordinary images of angels that fill the universe, we begin to move into a new level of consciousness in which we can experience the Divine Presence in virtually everything we engage. Our lives can become filled with a vast array of heavenly sparks that inform us of the divinity within even the most mundane activities. This is how I work with angels; it is an awesome and exciting experience. Come and see for yourself how to invoke angels with the methods described in this book and discover a new way to experience your world.

A Note on Gender: Each language has distinct limitations. A common practice in English is to refer to God in the masculine form: "He" or "Him." It is a problem that I have attempted to address. God has no gender, and the best we can do within the limits of our language is to use the pronoun "It," which frankly has its own deficiencies.

Angels also are without gender, but they have many different names. It is natural for us to associate a name with a gender. Thus, we find ourselves assuming that certain angels are masculine or feminine because of their names.

While I continue to be rigorous in referring to God-names in neutral terms, a rigid adherence to this rule when it comes to angels would often make a sentence structure cumbersome and pedantic. Therefore, I have been more concerned with the "feel" of the language and am comfortable going along with the gender assumptions of angels connected with various names. Still, be advised that even though I often use masculine or feminine pronouns when referring to angels, it should *not* be assumed that they are understood in the source texts to have a gender. ❖

Introduction

ONE OF MY most significant encounters with angels occurred in Jerusalem on December 31, 1990. The winters are chilly in Jerusalem, and many homes do not have central heating. My wife, Shoshana, and I lived in a two-story apartment with a large storage heater filled with bricks in the downstairs living room. Most of the heat naturally flowed up the stairwell, but the heater was far too heavy to move to a different location. After a number of chilly winters in our living room, I realized that a ceiling fan needed to be installed at the top of the stairs.

The upstairs ceiling was quite high, and I needed to balance with one foot on the railing of the stairs, leaning away from the ladder as I installed a toggle bolt for the fan. I wanted to be certain that the bolt would hold the heavy fan, so I tested it by hanging from it with my full weight, not considering what might happen if, in fact, the bolt did not hold me. Even to this day I remember a clear warning somewhere in the depths of my consciousness. I heard it, and ignored it. (We will see in the upcoming story of Balaam how easy it is to be blind to obvious signals.)

The primary building materials in the Old City are stone, marble, iron, and plaster. As the bolt broke loose from the plastered ceiling, I felt myself toppling over, about to fall headfirst to the bottom of the marble stairs. My instinct was to reach back for the rail or ladder as the weight of my body was falling in the opposite direction. In that instant, a voice distinctly cried out: "You must jump for the middle of the stairwell!"

It was counterintuitive to jump, but within a split second I realized that it was now or never; I only had a toehold left. So I jumped. I was able to land halfway down the stairs on one foot instead of falling out of control the full distance, which almost certainly would have resulted in a major injury. Instead, only my heel was crushed—broken into a few dozen pieces.

The moment I hit the uncarpeted marble floor, I knew something was wrong with my foot. But at that same instant I had the most enormous wave of relief wash over me. I was alive and not crippled! Except for the foot, I felt fine. It could have been far more serious. I found myself feeling the deepest sense of gratitude, almost euphoria, for the rest of that evening—despite the trip to the hospital, the pain, and the slow response of the physicians.

In that state of mind, throughout the evening I felt and knew clearly the surrounding and protective forces that people call angels. This was the first time I truly experienced an extraordinary, palpable sense of Presence, and I have returned to that experience many times over the years. It was not a visual experience of beings with wings, but rather a profound *knowing* that transcends the intellect.

Mystics over the ages have attempted to describe this feeling, but it defies words. Let me simply say that most of us have experienced the excitement and joy of anticipation when we are about to meet a beloved person, and most of us have experienced the deep pleasure at certain times when our beloved is sitting next to us. These experiences are similarly impossible to convey fully with words. The palpable sense of Presence is like the profound joy and pleasure of being held in the arms of a beloved; it elicits a peace of mind that transcends description.

My studies in Jerusalem often brought me in touch with realities beyond the ordinary mundane world. It is as if I put on glasses tinted with a certain hue, and everything is seen in that new way. With special glasses in place in the spiritual realm, the world fills up with angels of all types, shapes, sizes, and energies. They are part of daily prayers, they show up in many of the biblical texts, they fill the commentaries on the texts, and they can be seen in virtually every act that is performed.

When my mother died, a few years before the stairwell incident, my older brother called to tell me the news. On the flight to California from Israel, I gazed out of the window and experienced not simply clouds and sky, but myriads of angels and my mother's spirit dancing everywhere I looked. She danced happily, finally released. This was an amazing experience. I am certain that had I not been studying biblical commentaries for years, it would have been unlikely to have had that experience on the way to my mother's funeral. Yet seeing Mom dancing with angels opened my heart. While I grieved the loss, I was happy for her; she was now free. This is one important way that learning to invoke angels can be of enormous value when difficult or tragic situations arise.

Living with angels on a daily basis cultivates an entirely new view. I do not experience angels in Hollywood images as beatific forms with wings. Rather, everything takes on a special quality; everything feels connected in a fascinating way. Whatever sense calls to me—sight, sound, touch, taste or smell—each sensation has a new feel to it. The puff of a breeze, the dance of a shadow, all shapes, movements, energies—each has a special quality. Moreover, when angels are invoked, there is a fascinating experience of never feeling alone. There is a sense of being in the midst of a constantly unfolding creation that is rich, awesome, brilliant, and complete; each and every moment is stunning.

A couple of months after breaking my heel, I got a call from my niece that my older brother had a nearly fatal heart attack. My niece is a physician, and she told me on the phone that he had about a one-in-ten chance of surviving. I caught the next plane out for New York and got to Syracuse as quickly as I could. On the way, I found myself doing a traditional archangel meditation, surrounding myself with the archangels: Michael, Gabriel, Raphael, and Uriel. My oldest brother's name is Ralph, and Raphael, as will be seen, is the archangel of healing.

I arrived at his bedside in the cardiac unit and saw all the tubes running in and out of his body. He could not speak because the machines were helping him breathe, but his recognition and his smile as I entered the room were priceless. When I got there, he demanded that the tube in his throat be removed, even though the risk was high. As they pulled the tube, I was in communion with the angel Raphael.

My brother survived and continues to do well fifteen years later. I do not talk to Ralph about the angel Raphael, for my brother does not want to hear about such things. His world, like that of so many, is not inhabited by angels;

even the word makes him cringe. So what? My invoking Raphael was as much for me as it was for Ralph.

I do not claim that my connection with this archangel was the cause for my brother's survival, yet I felt that both of us were "helped." I gained strength and conviction, and nobody knows to what extent this kind of conscious support and prayer for healing is useful. Still, faced with the choice between feeling entirely helpless, or using the tools of angelic imagery and prayer, I am drawn to calling upon a mysterious force of healing in which I find relief and comfort.

I have found that the archangel prayer is one of the most powerful ways to cultivate a kind of intimacy with the angelic realm. Its extraordinary power has been revealed to me time and again as I assist people in my role as a rabbi in situations of great stress, especially in times of illness or serious accidents or when I work with someone who is dying.

In the mid-nineties I was contacted by a dear friend whose son had just been seriously injured in a freak accident. He had a head injury that was causing swelling of the brain and spinal cord, and the outlook was not good. When we spoke, the surgeons had induced a coma to relieve the pressure in the hope that the swelling could be controlled. By phone, I taught my friend the archangel prayer and meditation as well as a melody that is often associated with it, and suggested that she do it out loud with her son as often as possible. Though my friend is Christian, the Archangel Meditation is universal, and people from all traditions can work with it comfortably.

She began immediately, talking and singing this guided meditation and prayer, despite the fact that her son was in a coma. She did this for days, virtually nonstop, except to sleep occasionally. When he finally came out of the coma, her son knew the words and melody of the prayer by heart; moreover, he reported visualizations of light-filled beings that he had experienced while unconscious. To this day, my friend is certain that archangels were invoked, and they saved her son.

In a story like this most of us focus on the healing power of the angels. I would like to draw attention to the fact that this mother put her heart and soul into the experience of invoking angels, which is a process that must not be ignored; it was clearly for her a vital part of the healing that took place. Moreover, the prayers offered her a refuge in which she could participate and find some solace during those anxious days while the boy was in a coma. Healing can occur on many levels in the practice of invoking angels.

In this book we are going to explore the world of angels, and we are going to learn a number of guided meditations. These meditations are designed to help you incorporate the practices of visualization and imagination in a way that becomes comfortable and familiar. Through repetition we in essence "befriend" certain qualities that are associated with different angels. In a short time we are able to invoke feelings that connect us with the desired characteristics.

While you will greatly strengthen your experience of the book by listening and following the guided instruction for meditation, it should be noted that the accompanying audio program is designed in a way that someone who may be unable to read the book for whatever reason can still benefit by simply listening to and following the audio guided meditations.

The first track of the CD contains the short form of the Archangel Meditation. Listen to this first track repeatedly until it is memorized. It is easy to learn. Learning it by heart will give you easy access to the spontaneous invocation of these archangels in various situations.

This very practice of the Archangel Meditation is done in observant Jewish households by children and adults alike, every evening before going to sleep. It becomes so ingrained as an evening practice that it automatically arises in difficult and challenging times.

Later in the book I will describe the specific characteristics of a number of angels, including all of those named in this meditation practice. Accordingly, the CD has a track with an extended version of the Archangel Meditation, which adds richness and power to the experience. For now, however, it is more useful to memorize the fundamental practice, as it is short and easy to learn.

At various times throughout the course of this book I will suggest that you stop reading for a while and work with some of the chants and practices that are offered on the accompanying CD. Please listen to the recorded tracks one at a time, and spend time with each, for the process of invoking angels is a technique that requires immersion and repetition.

Enjoy yourself. The angelic realm is a wondrous world of infinite possibilities. So let us now begin to explore the world of angels as we know them in the Western tradition. Relax and let yourself go into the process. ❖

LISTEN TO TRACK 1
Archangel Meditation
(short form)

PART ONE

A Mystical Understanding
of Angels

ANGELS AND HUMANS

In a famous biblical episode, Jacob wrestles a "man" who, when he realizes that he cannot defeat Jacob, touches Jacob's thigh and throws it out of joint (Gen. 32:26). All oral commentaries agree that Jacob's opponent was not an ordinary man, but an angel. There are thousands of biblical commentaries, including the Talmud, the oral tradition (Midrash), the mystical tradition (Zohar and Kabbalah), and the Hasidic tradition, as well as those in Christianity and Islam, that describe and discuss angels. In our modern times, one can Google the words "angel" and "angels" and get a combined number of over one hundred million hits, suggesting that angels are a subject of considerable interest to many people in the world.

It is fascinating to note, for example, that when the Dalai Lama met Rabbi Zalman Schachter-Shalomi, as described in the book *The Jew in the Lotus,* the Buddhist leader was enthralled by the Jewish perspective on angels. A detailed discussion between Reb Zalman and the Dalai Lama on the angels of different traditions ensued. Many of the deities in the Tibetan world have almost exactly the same characteristics as certain archangels in the Western world. Moreover, these characteristics are cultivated by using similar contemplative methods of visualization for protection, healing, blessing, strength, support, wisdom, compassion, and lovingkindness.

The angelic realm is vast; it is a new way of looking at things. We learn in the Jewish oral tradition, for example, that God consulted angels before creating humans. In these teachings, angels were not too excited about creating a human species, for they could see that it was destined to cause great trouble in the universe. It is also taught that angels were generally "jealous" of humans because we were destined to have greater latitude in our expression of free will. Angels have only limited free will, as they are more intimately connected with the Divine; humans have extensive free will, and we are more easily confused about the purpose of our own existence. These teachings provide a mythos for encountering the world in a different way.

We find that God also "consults" with humans. For example, Abraham argues with God about the decision to destroy Sodom, and he negotiates with God to try to save the city. Of course, we learn later that the city is destroyed. The issue is not what God "knew" in advance, rather it is the revelation of an interaction, a debate, and a give and take between Abraham and God (Gen. 18:24–32).

We see the same process many times between Moses and God. Moses continually attempts to dissuade God from wiping out the Israelites for being so stiff-necked and hardheaded. The ability to argue with God opens an entirely new way to relate to the predicament of our existence.

Prophets, like Jonah, argue with God. Hasidic masters, like Levi Yitzhak of Berdichev, constantly challenge God. Indeed, we are actually invited to confront God and angels. This is a very different perspective from the widespread view that the human relationship to the Source should be one of complete subservience and total surrender.

Angels, on the other hand, only occasionally argue with God. Even the "fallen angels" who have a primary role in adding to the confusion of humans still need God's "permission" to act, as we will see later. So angels are intermediaries between the unknowable force of creation—the center of life—and every aspect of the manifest universe. Indeed, their relationship to God is different from that of humans.

It is taught in many places that the creation of humans was never in doubt; rather, God's consulting with angels is to point out the liabilities of free will. Theoretically, this world would run beautifully if humans did not exercise their own self-interest. However, as we humans are part of nature, the extensive and often troublesome free will we have is viewed by the Jewish sages as a great experiment.

The experiment is this: can humans as co-creators (with extensive free will) cultivate a world that is more profound and on a higher level of perfection than a world of angels (with limited free will) without humans? This presents humans with a significant challenge: we must realize that we are not only permitted, but indeed obliged, to do whatever is in our power to try to improve the way life unfolds, even when it involves "arguing" with God in a way that will influence, and in fact change, the way things happen.

THE SOURCE OF LIFE

If someone throws a ball and it crashes through a window, do we say that the ball broke the window or that the person throwing the ball broke the window? Clearly, the primary mover is the source of the movement, and the responsibility falls to this source. The ball did not break the window of its own volition—it was thrown.

There is a deeper aspect to this question. Did the person throwing the ball break the window, or was there a primary mover behind this person—did God break the window? There is a considerable range of opinions concerning the meaning of the word "God." What is God? How does God function? What role does God play in everyday events? Can God be influenced through our actions, thoughts, or prayers?

Without losing ourselves in a theological discussion, I would like to explain that when I use the word *God,* I am referring to the force of life that is continuously unfolding from moment to moment. There are no implications in this context that refer to creation, morality, behavior, or the principle of good and evil. The main interest we have here is how life, nature, and the cosmos arise in this instant, and how this natural process of unending change causes the universe to be completely different each and every moment.

In this framework, the creative force that brings about the urge for life is the same force that sustains the motion of every atomic particle and every wave in the universe. This is not a question of belief: it is a simple fact of physics that every bit of matter in this universe has motion; nothing exists without motion. I choose to call the essential organizing principle behind the motion of the universe *God-ing*. Kabbalists refer to the ultimate Source as *Ein Sof* (without end), which means "boundlessness." This is not a thing, not a noun, not a being—but a verb, a process, an unending *now-ness*. The reader who is interested in exploring this in greater depth can find an expanded explanation in my work *God Is a Verb*.

This idea of God as a *process* opens a new understanding of the point made earlier about the role of humans in arguing with God. We might have thought about this in dualistic terms—that we humans would complain and argue with a separate God who was in ultimate control of things. With God as process, however, we humans are an integral part of that process; we are not separate. In this instance, *our complaints or disagreements are actually an expression of the Divine;* they are part of the shaping of creation from moment to moment. Indeed, our free will and the way it is expressed is a vital element that makes us co-creators of the universe, an integral part of the God-ing process.

So the answer to the question of whether the stone thrower or God broke the window is that *one cannot be separated from the other.* The stone thrower is an expression of the Divine; it does not act as a separate entity. The window is broken, and it is also not separate. Windows break when hit by stones—this is the nature of glass. We must change our linear thinking to the understanding of Oneness, that each unfolding moment is the expression of the Divine.

Everything that "is" and everything that happens is an expression of God-ing. We do not need to await the touch of the Divine in order to know this; we simply need to open our eyes and our ears to experience what is happening right here and right now. We cannot separate ourselves from the God-ing expression; it is constantly happening. It is as close to us as our own breath and our own heartbeats; indeed, it is us, our actions, and even our thoughts.

The God-ing process is vast and all-encompassing; we cannot grasp its magnitude. It is not limited by infinity. We cannot even imagine infinity, let alone the idea of something bigger than infinity. So when we say that the God-ing process is infinity to the power of infinity, we are establishing clearly that it is beyond imagination, beyond the mind, and that it is therefore absurd to attempt to understand the meaning of God-ing. It includes, but is not limited to, all universes, all realities, and all possibilities, from the smallest to the largest. Yet, amazingly, we can settle into it and "know" it on a level beyond the mind. In essence, we can learn to recognize Presence as it is, and we can learn to immerse ourselves in it without trying to hold on to it. Dwelling in Presence, we become mystics.

HAPPENINGS AND MIRACLES

There is an order to the universe, both in terms of our scientific understanding of the laws of physics and in terms of our ordinary daily experience of nature. We all know that a fish out of water will soon die; we do not need physics to explain it. Moreover, the fish out of water is our metaphor for anything out of its place in the "natural" flow of things.

The natural flow, the unfolding of each moment, follows a series of laws that give this continuous flow orderliness and, to some extent, predictability. Higher science often determines events in the context of probabilities. While all events can be viewed through a lens of scientific inquiry, they can also be experienced in more mystical terms, as processes operating on many planes.

The realm of angels is built upon a fundamental assumption: everything that exists is an expression of a life-giving force that is indescribable, unknowable, and boundless. Anything we try to think about with regard to this is, by definition, less than it. Comparing the thinking mind to Ein Sof

(Boundlessness) is like comparing the width of a razor's edge to the distance of a trillion light-years.

The mind, however, does experience each moment as it unfolds. It experiences reality in its own unique way, coloring incidents with its own conditioning, its predilections, its judgments, desires, dislikes, and so forth. Still, we experience life as we see it, in a wide variety of happenings. When our minds try to explain how things happen and why things happen, we come up with many ideas. If an event goes beyond anything that fits our natural way of seeing things, we put it into a category of a miraculous happening.

Actually, a great deal of life is inexplicable, and small miracles abound. Life itself is a miracle. The ordinary happenings of everyday experiences—our health, our relationships, our food, our shelter—these abundances are enormous. Usually we do not fully recognize the nature of these small miracles until one of them disappears. Once gone, however, we suddenly realize how casual and nonchalant we are about the necessities of life that nurture us and protect us every day.

Ironically, most miracles work in hidden ways. When a fast-moving automobile has a front tire blow, for example, and we are fifty feet ahead of or behind that car as it swerves out of control, this "near miss" is a big miracle. Had we been alongside the car when it began to swerve out of control, anything could have happened. Do we notice that? Do we call it a miracle? Can we say our guardian angel was watching over us?

When the full airplane does *not* have engine failure, when the jammed holiday cruise ship stays steady in a storm, when the crowded building does not burst into flames, we think nothing of it. It is natural to assume things will go fine all the time. Only later might someone discover a loose fuel line that could easily have exploded in the airplane's engine, or an almost-sheared pin on the engine shaft of the boat that if broken would have caused a dangerous loss of control in the storm, or the leak in the gas main of the building discovered just in time—these are all miracles that go unnoticed.

We read in our daily newspapers or see on television all the times when there were no hidden miracles and tragedies resulted. But for every event in the news, there are unrecorded millions of potential events that never happen. When things go well, as they most often do, it is a powerful experience to consider our good fortune. When we do, we cannot help but be enormously grateful. In this gratitude, we automatically open our hearts and minds to the marvel of hidden blessings of both big and small miracles that fill our lives. This daily gratitude is a major step in connecting ourselves with the hidden, unknown realms of fate and fortune that continually play a dramatic role in our everyday lives.

THE WISE GUIDE MEDITATION

Let us now work a little more with our imaginations. As we develop more skills in imagining things, we learn better how to cultivate certain mind states. This process helps us to recondition our own minds. The first step in becoming acquainted with angels is to learn how to play with our imaginations. We are actually experts in imagining things; we do it all the time. When we are thinking about something that happened in the past, or pondering something that may happen in the future, we are imagining. It can become so real for us and so powerful that we physically and emotionally respond to the imagination arising in our minds.

The meditative method of cultivation is to purposely guide our imaginations into areas that will evoke desirable responses and feelings. We will work with various guided meditations as we move through the teachings offered in this book.

Keep in mind that imagination works in different ways for different people. Some of us are quite visual, and we see distinct images in our minds. Some of us have strong connections with sounds, smells, or bodily sensations. Many people simply "think" an idea without any particular sensory experience, but they relate to concepts and words. All these different ways can be used for powerful experiences involving imagination.

Please listen to Track 2 on the accompanying CD for a basic exercise in imagination. If you have difficulty at first, do not hesitate to play the track over again a number of times. Despite the fact that we use imagination all the time, people are often initially resistant to guided meditations. However, once we relax into the process, we find considerable creativity and distinctive powers of imagination that rapidly arise when invited. See what you discover in this exercise. (Please have a diary or some blank paper when you begin, as it helps to keep a record of your experiences.)

LISTEN TO TRACK 2
Wise Guide Meditation

TYPES OF ANGELS

There are angels of all types: messengers, ministers, accusers, guardians, archangels, teachers, assistants, and so forth. The most "ordinary" type of angel is a messenger, and the most prevalent message is simply "Be." Whereas on the microcosmic level there are angels for the smallest form of matter, on the macrocosmic level there are angels for forests, mountains, seas, nations, the Moon, the Sun, the solar system, celestial bodies, galaxies, and constellations—there is an angel for everything, large or small, in the universe.

Angels are not limited to this universe alone, and they span the various heavens and hells and all that is outside of our limited understanding of time and space. The view of the ancient sages was that the harmonies and disharmonies of the universe were all forms of divine expression. That is to say that everything that happens in the universe is an expression of God, and all of these expressions are carried out by angels.

Some angels last only momentarily, long enough to carry a short message; other angels are long lasting. For example, eternal angels called Ofanim, Seraphim, and Hayyot attend to the highest throne in the heavenly realms. There are also well-known archangels like Michael, Gabriel, Raphael, and Uriel, who are also eternal. There are additional eternal heavenly figures, such as Metatron, Sandalphon, and Elijah, about whom we will learn.

The Talmud teaches that every individual has a guardian angel. Every person also has an angel of destiny. There is some debate as to whether these are two separate angels or one. It is taught that angels, especially guardian angels, communicate with the soul when the body is asleep. The main methods of communication are dreams, visions, and prophetic insights. Whether this communication takes place when one is asleep or awake, the prophets usually referred to an interior voice, something from "within," rather than an outer voice.

A very popular Talmudic teaching in traditional Judaism says that two angels accompany a person to his or her home on the Sabbath eve: one is good and one is evil. If the house is set with a beautiful table and is well prepared to receive the Sabbath, then the good angel makes a blessing: "May this house be like this as well for the Sabbath to come." In this instance, the evil angel must unwillingly say, "Amen," as if it agreed with this blessing. On the other hand, if the house is unclean, messy, and unprepared, then the reverse happens; the evil angel says the same blessing, and the good angel must agree with, "Amen."

The Talmud says that ministering angels are created out of a stream of fire. They sing—that is to say, they do their assigned task—and then they disappear. Another interpretation is that every physical movement in the universe is considered an "utterance" of God, and, moreover, every movement in the universe is accompanied by a new angel. It is also said that when someone prays in earnest, the angels that accompany this person embrace and purify him or her.

Angels are considered to be almost infinite in number; they are omnipresent. The hosts of angels fill the heavens and every firmament. Almost all angels dwell in another reality and are invisible in the ordinary world. However, some make themselves visible at times. In kabbalistic terms, if we had the eyes to see the truth of creation, we would realize that everything we see or experience is actually an angel covering or containing a divine spark within it. But most of the time we fail to recognize what we experience for what it really is. In fact, one of the hidden kabbalistic teachings is that the word *garment* secretly means *angel.* That is to say, the covering of everything, its form, can be considered a garment. Once we recognize the true nature of garments, we will recognize that everything has an intrinsic value and a spark of the Divine. Recognizing the depths of this truth, we will realize that everything we engage in in our daily activities and in our own minds is actually an expression of God.

With all this, it is important to emphasize that angels act only as intermediaries or messengers of the God-ing process. They should never be viewed as divine creatures who in any way could act on their own in place of God. Angels in many ways are flawed, just as are humans. They are not omniscient;

they can be tricked or confused and are even incapable of answering certain questions. Some have been cast out of one of the heavens for making mistakes. Certain angels are "fallen," and their dominion is the Dark Side, that which opposes the light of awareness. It is these very imperfections that allow the possibility of human interaction, for if everything were clearly illuminated and there were no confusion about how the universe unfolds, then we would not be able to express free will.

So we find that angels can plead for themselves, and they can plead for humans. There are accusing angels, created by our misdeeds, as well as defending angels, created by our good deeds. Many Hasidic tales take us to the heavenly courts where accusing and defending angels battle for a person's soul, and often the ultimate decision is based on a single angel who tips the scales. It is a powerful experience to move through life knowing our fate may be hanging on the balance of a single deed committed at any time.

Some humans are under the custody of angels, some are equal with angels, and some actually *become* angels, as we will see later with the biblical figures of Enoch and Elijah. Still, we are cautioned never to forget that even when angels are carrying our prayers, there is only one source of life—Ein Sof, Boundlessness, which ultimately determines our fate.

Thus, we can use angels, work with angels, be guided or assisted by angels, but never worship them. In essence, we treat angels as special friends who have great powers as well as having interesting "connections." There is no assurance that they will accomplish what we want, but there is an enormous value in having them on our side, so to speak. The Dark Side, often called the Other Side, that automatically opposes us has considerable powers of confusion and will always be present, uninvited, attempting to "do its job." This is the mystery and awe of entering the world of angels.

THE GOOD INCLINATION VERSUS
THE NOT-GOOD INCLINATION

It is taught in the Jewish tradition that two angels accompany a person throughout life, a *yetzer ha-tov* (good inclination) and a *yetzer ha-ra* (not-good inclination). What does it mean to be drawn toward the good or away from it? From a mystical perspective, it means to engage in activities that awaken one's higher consciousness—to come closer to the truth of existence—or to do those things that keep us immersed in confusion and ignorance. These two angels are always tugging against each other.

We constantly experience this inner tension in our daily activities. Some activities clearly bring us to higher levels of consciousness, and some do the opposite. Most of our encounters with life, however, are in a gray area that does not clearly take us one way or the other. In this context the teaching is quite explicit. When we have a choice and are determined to move ourselves toward the good, the yetzer ha-tov gains power over the yetzer ha-ra. If we do this with regular frequency, the good side develops a momentum that pulls us, subconsciously and automatically, toward the good. Of course, the opposite is true, and not-good decisions can also develop a momentum. We learn from this an important lesson: our smallest deeds, be they in harmony or disharmony with life, carry energy that leads us along paths that tend to follow more harmony or disharmony.

Each time we make small choices that lead us in the direction of the not-good—perhaps the extra portion of rich food or the time we spend with the television or neglecting our most important relationships—we empower the yetzer ha-ra, and we find ourselves more often in its grip of disharmony without knowing how we got there. Conversely, when we pay close attention to small details, such as that extra phone call to someone in need or the extra contributions to charity or the special time we take simply to nurture ourselves—the dozens and dozens of possibilities to empower the harmonies of the yetzer ha-tov—we find our lives moving with greater ease and less complication, and we generally find ourselves more in balance with life.

The teachings suggest that the angel of the not-good inclination attaches itself to an infant when it is born and is active throughout early childhood. This is why we do not hold children responsible for their actions; they don't really know any better. However, at a certain level of maturity, around twelve or thirteen years of age, the child becomes capable of making wiser choices, and this is when the angel of the yetzer ha-tov comes into his or her life. Good parenting is knowing when and how to guide the child toward the good inclination; in other words, the good parent actually acts out and establishes the role of the yetzer ha-tov angel long before it arrives. In this way, the angel of the yetzer ha-ra does not gain too much power during those early years.

More important in the long run is how each of us works with our own good and not-good inclinations. It is never too late to begin nurturing the good inclination that resides within us. One notices very quickly the results of intentional activities to raise consciousness. The yetzer ha-tov becomes a "happy" angel, and we can actually feel this harmonious experience—as will be demonstrated in the upcoming exercise.

Interestingly, the teachings also suggest that the not-good angel actually does not want to fully succeed! In a way, it actually "wants" to be defeated. So it does not fight us when we make the choice for good; indeed, it bows to us and it joins "hands" with the yetzer ha-tov to guard us in our lives. In this context, the oral tradition quotes Psalms 91:11–12: "It will give angels to protect you, to watch over you in everything you do. They will hold you in their hands, so that you do not hurt your foot on a stone." This means that by strengthening the good angel, both the good and the not-good angels will protect you so that you are able to stay out of harm's way even when you do not see it coming.

There is an interesting Talmudic teaching that says "Even if there are a thousand accusing angels [for the thousand misdeeds one has done], only one angel vouching for a person's goodness will be sufficient to redeem this person." One of the sages of the Talmud, Rabbi Abba, questions this teaching. He asks why God should need an angel to affirm one's goodness, when God already knows everything about this person. In Talmudic fashion, the solution to this inquiry is that the one angel who vouches for a person's good is not just any angel, but is specifically the yetzer ha-ra, the not-good angel, who has been won over by the good deeds of someone to the point where this angel essentially becomes the person's primary defender. Thus, the teaching is that although it is obvious to God that a person is good at the core, it is of great significance when a not-good angel admits defeat.

The leader of the yetzer ha-tov angels is the archangel Gabriel; the leader of the yetzer ha-ra angels is Samael, who was the serpent that seduced Eve. Samael is also considered to be the father of Cain as well as the tempter of Abraham. Samael is best known as Satan. Thus, the description above gives us insight into the limits of the power of satanic and demonic forces, according to the ancient sages. Not only are these forces potentially subservient to the forces of good, they can be made into allies in the challenge to move to higher levels of consciousness. This is fundamental in the Hasidic teachings, which say that at the heart of everything is a spark of the Divine, including the heart of so-called evil.

By working with angels and moving in the direction of the yetzer ha-tov, represented by Gabriel, we bring both sides together and thus bring all of humanity increasingly closer to higher and higher consciousness. Learning how to do this with wisdom and compassion is one of the primary challenges on the spiritual path.

While the dominant archangel of the good inclination, the yetzer ha-tov, is Gabriel, we have noted that each individual is said to have his or her own personal guardian angel. This angel within each of us can be experienced by observing our own minds, feelings and reactions in various situations. How do we respond, what draws us, what is our immediate inclination as we engage different people and changing events? The inner experience of our own tendencies reveals to each of us the inclinations of our own personal angels.

Oftentimes things are happening so quickly that we simply react without paying attention to the implications of our actions. One of the benefits of meditation practice is that we can imagine situations and observe our own behavior as if the visualization were real. We have all experienced physical reactions when we are deeply engaged in some imaginary scene. In the same way, we can invite specific visualizations and learn a great deal by the way the guided visualization unfolds in our minds. Let us see how this works in the Guardian Angel Meditation. ◈

LISTEN TO TRACK 3
Guardian Angel Meditation

PART TWO

Angels in the Bible

THE TORAH

In the Torah—the Five Books of Moses, often referred to as the Old Testament—we find fascinating references to angels. There is an angel in the story of God directing Abraham to sacrifice his son, Isaac. An angel stops Abraham at the last moment from committing the act (Gen. 22:11–12). This was seen as a test that Abraham had to pass, and of course this story has been of profound interest to readers over many centuries.

When Abraham sent his servant Eliezer to seek out a wife for his son Isaac, Eliezer was guided by an angel to Rebecca. Eliezer told Rebecca specifically that he had been guided to her by an angel, which was evidence that convinced Rebecca that her intended soulmate was indeed Isaac (Gen. 24:40).

In yet another well-known story, Isaac's son Jacob has a dream of angels ascending and descending a ladder that spanned the distance between heaven and earth (Gen. 28:12). In this story, God promises Jacob—who is running for his life—that he will be protected and that he will be the father of the nation promised to his own father, Isaac, and his grandfather, Abraham. When Jacob awakens from this dream, he pronounces in his awe: "God is here and I did not know it!" (Gen. 28:16). This is a crucial mystical teaching that says, *God is always here, if we only have the eyes to see.*

Jacob sets up a pillar to mark this spot, anoints it with oil, and names the place Beth-El, the house of God. A few chapters later, Jacob recounts that he was visited in another dream by an angel who gave him a vision and then declared, "I am the God of Beth-El ..." (Gen. 31:11–13). This interface between angels who act as messengers and those who identify themselves as God happens on numerous occasions in the Torah, to the point where one cannot help but wonder how to clearly distinguish between the two.

Indeed, the Torah frequently uses pronouns in such a way that we do not know who is speaking. This is particularly true when there is an interaction between a primary biblical character and God. Commentators have a great deal to say about these ambiguities, and they often become major teaching points. When we do not know whether it is God or an angel who is speaking, we still know that the angel is only acting as a messenger. The deeper we explore these kinds of questions, the more we resolve and understand that all things and all actions are interconnected, and all eventually arise from and return to Boundlessness, the Source of Being.

Jacob has other encounters with angels. In one, the ordinary translation is "... angels of God met him" (Gen. 32:2). The mystical interpretation for this verse focuses on the use of the Hebrew word *bo*—meaning "in"—that indicates that the literal translation should read: ". . . angels of God met *in* him." This new reading suggests that Jacob regularly experienced angels in his inner vision, and thus he epitomizes the ultimate mystical experience of continuously living in Presence.

A few more well-known mentions of angels in the Torah include the episode of the blessing of Joseph's sons by their grandfather Jacob, who also goes by the name of Israel (Gen. 48:14–16). An angel is invoked in this blessing. The episode of Moses at the burning bush has an angel appearing to him out of the flame, and then God speaks to him directly (Ex. 3:2). There is an angel who accompanies and protects the Israelites on their flight out of Mitzrayim (Ex. 14:19) (which is normally translated as "Egypt," but should more correctly be referred to as "a place of constriction"). There is an angel with the Israelites during their forty years in the desert. Simply said, angels appear, one way or another, in almost every significant Bible story.

Direct, explicit references to angels in the Torah use Hebrew words like *malach yhvh.* Malach means "messenger" in Hebrew, and the Hebrew letters "yhvh" represent the tetragrammaton. This is one of the most important names of God, never pronounced, but usually rendered in Hebrew as *Ado-noy,* or translated into English as "the Lord." Thus, malach yhvh is commonly read, "angel of the Lord," and this reference appears many times in the books of Genesis, Exodus, and Numbers. In addition, references to angels can be found dozens of times in other parts of the Bible: in Judges, Samuel, Kings, Isaiah, Hoshea, Zacharia, Psalms, Job, Ecclesiastes, Daniel, and Chronicles.

THE STORY OF BALAAM

The final time we dramatically encounter an angel in the written tradition of the Torah is in the story of Balaam and his donkey, who are en route to put a curse on the Israelites (Num. 22). It was known that Balaam had powerful magic and that his curse could drive anyone from the land. This is a mysterious story in the Torah, and it has evoked an enormous amount of commentary. As it is one of the most revelatory biblical stories concerning the nature of angels, let us explore it more closely.

The Israelites wandered in the desert for forty years. In so doing, they encountered various tribes who were settled on the land. Some of these encounters were peaceful, and some were not. In the case of the Moabites, Balak, the king, was afraid that the Israelites would be hostile. So he sent his elders to summon the sage, Balaam, who was well versed in the arts of the occult, to put a curse on the potential enemies.

When approached by these elders, Balaam asked them to stay the night so that he could use his magic to ask God (Elohim) what to do. When God appeared to him that night, Balaam reported the request by Balak that he curse the nation of the Israelites. God's response was that Balaam should not go with these men, and he should not curse the nation in question because it was already a blessed nation. So in the morning Balaam sent the elders back to King Balak with his refusal.

Balak, however, was insistent. He sent another group, this one larger and with higher rank, with the message that Balaam was to come, whatever the cost. Balaam replied that no amount of wealth would be sufficient to violate the word of God. Nonetheless, Balaam still asked his visitors to stay the night to see what God would say to him the second time around. This time, God said that Balaam could go with these men, but advised him to do only what God instructed him to do.

The next morning, Balaam hurried to saddle his donkey and went with the delegation. At this point the story turns quite mysterious. In the very section of the Torah in which God tells Balaam he can go, the language of the Torah continues "And God's anger glowed because he went" (Num. 22). The reader is left to wonder why God would be angry after having already given Balaam the okay to go. While there are many interpretations for this story, the commentaries generally agree that Balaam was obviously anxious to go for the selfish reasons of fame and fortune. He already had his answer from God and had no need to check a second time. In spite of God's instructions, Balaam was trying to find a way to do the task requested by Balak.

The message here is that although Balaam had occult powers, and even though he was careful in his use of these powers, he could also be corrupted by status and wealth. So he looked for a loophole, so to speak, in the earlier instructions. He had a personal agenda and was not completely open to divine guidance.

When God's anger is revealed, it says that "an angel of God placed itself in the way to block [Balaam]" (Num. 22:22), but Balaam and the others with him did not see this angel. Only the donkey upon which Balaam was riding saw this angel. Facing this awesome, threatening angel holding a raised sword, the donkey swerved off the road into an adjoining field. Balaam, still blind to the angel, beat the animal to get her back to the road. They moved onto a narrow path in the adjoining vineyard.

The angel, still with a raised sword, blocked the way on this new path as well. The donkey leaned to one side, trying to avoid the angel, accidentally crushing Balaam's foot on the fence. Balaam beat the animal even more. Unfortunately, the path was so narrow that there was no room to move either left or right. At this point, when the donkey saw the angel again, she lay down and would not move. Balaam was enraged, and he beat her once again with a stick.

This animal had seen the angel three times; Balaam had not seen it at all. Even with all his powers and ability to commune with God, Balaam was so focused on his own inner world that he was oblivious to what was happening around him. At this point in the story, we cannot help but wonder why he was unable to realize the presence of the angel. Why was the angel revealed only to the donkey?

Now the story becomes quite strange, for the donkey is given the power of speech! She asks Balaam, "What have I done to you that you beat me three times?" (Num. 22:28) Balaam shouts, "You have rebelled against me. If I had a sword, I would kill you!" She replies, "Am I not your donkey that you have always ridden from the beginning until now? Have I ever done this to you before?" And he says, "No" (Num. 22:30).

The fact that the donkey can talk is astonishing. It raises difficult issues, particularly on the subject of how this world operates. Is it a world in which anything can happen, or is there some order, some universal law that cannot be broken? In our modern view, we are not as astonished about these kinds of things. We see many strange phenomena in science, and some of us might even remember Mr. Ed, the talking horse, from television. For the ancient sages, however, a talking donkey sparked an inquiry into the nature of the universe. They went so far as to say that Balaam's donkey was a one-time-only miracle, created before creation itself, in order to do exactly what she did in this encounter with Balaam, and then to die, never to be heard from again.

This incident in the Torah invites us into a philosophical and theological discussion that could easily lead us astray from our theme. With regard to angels, however, it is a marvelous teaching story. We learn from it that there are many realities. Each individual carries his or her own reality, depending upon the conditioning of that person's mind. This is why it is difficult to get witnesses to a single event to agree on exactly how the event unfolded. In addition, there is a reality shaped by our intellect, another shaped by our emotions, another that is a function of our perceptions, and so on. Our realities are also constructed by our beliefs, our judgments, and our self-awareness. In addition, it is clear that animals, insects, and other life forms have their own unique views of reality.

Balaam was such an advanced practitioner of the occult arts that he could invite an encounter with a reality in which he could commune with God. Yet he was unable to experience an angelic presence that his own donkey could perceive. He was blinded by his own desires and his lack of humility. The instant Balaam was able to realize that his donkey did not deserve the beatings, he gained greater perspective. At that point he gets his "eyes opened" (Num. 22:31). With the ability to see in a new way, Balaam is finally able to perceive the angel with the drawn sword, and he is so shocked he falls on his face—a sign of profound awe.

Now the angel repeats the question the donkey had asked: "Why did you beat this beloved donkey who has served you so well?" When the Torah repeats something, it is driving a point home. This is our lesson. When we are lost in our own beliefs and our personal motivations, we miss what is really happening around us. The angel goes on to say, "If your donkey had not turned aside, I would have killed you!" (Num. 22:33)

Balaam is filled with remorse and reflects that if God considers it wrong to do this task, he will return home—but this was already clear from the start. Now things have changed. When he asks yet again, he is still told to go, but "do not say anything other than the exact words I say to you." (Eventually we see that instead of cursing the Israelites, Balaam ends up blessing them.)

Thus Balaam has come full circle, and in so doing he is now in direct contact with the angelic presence. He is no longer functioning on his own agenda; he has truly become a vehicle for the expression of the Divine. This is a powerful teaching that opens gateways for working with the presence of angels. It is interesting to note that the word for angel in Hebrew (*malach*) is written eleven times in this section on Balaam, more than in any other single section of the Bible. ❖

PART THREE

The Main Archangels

ANGELOLOGY

Angelology, the study of angels, has always been of particular interest to mystics. They believe that the more we understand about how angels function, the more we will be able to interact and work with them. Some of the earliest known mystics in the Jewish tradition were the Essenes, who are closely associated with the Dead Sea Scrolls that were discovered in the area known as Qumran. These mystics believed in an elaborate system of guardian angels that were represented as heavenly princes.

In addition to mystics, who often worked with contemplative practices to evoke angels, cultures in many parts of the world have been intrigued by angelic forces. The idea that there are ways to communicate with something beyond our own reality has a fascination that has sparked human inquiry over all of recorded history. Indeed, when we compile references to different angels, there are thousands of names that appear. There are strange names such as Zagzagael, who was revealed to Moses in the burning bush; Dubiel, the guardian angel of the Persians; Gezardiya, the guardian angel in charge of everything in the Eastern direction; Pesagniyah, the angel in charge of the South; Petahyah, the angel of the North; Zebuliel, the chief angel of the West; Kafziel and Hizkiel, chief angels under the archangel Gabriel; and Zophiel and Zadkiel, chief angels under the archangel Michael. The list continues on and on.

As mentioned earlier, we will center our inquiry and our meditations on a small number of the angels most frequently mentioned in the oral tradition, including archangels Michael, Gabriel, Raphael, Uriel, and the special angels Metatron, Sandalphon, and Elijah. We will also take a detailed look at the Angel of Death, as well as the Shekhina, who represents the Divine Presence. Each of these angelic archetypes has unique qualities, and, as we will see, each can be called upon to imbue an individual with certain powers.

An important note to remember: The work in which you are about to engage has enormous potential. Treat it with respect and care. You will find that the techniques we describe function on many levels, as long as you approach your own potential for imagination with an open mind and a willingness of heart.

ANGELS EVERYWHERE

It is said that every blade of grass has an angel hovering over it, calling to it, saying: "Grow!" The instant an angel does its task of calling forth the urge to grow, it immediately fades away. In the next moment another angel appears over the blade of grass, and it calls out, "Grow!" Then, it too instantly disappears, and yet another and another and another angel appears, fresh in every moment, urging the grass to grow!

Thus, every single blade of grass has untold trillions of angels attending it, urging it to live. So too every leaf, every living being, and indeed every atom has its angels urging it to move, to fly, to be whatever it is. Yes, even every wave, every vibration, every nuance of this universe has its mystery that can be described in angelic terms. In this context, almost all angels are expressions of life and creation; they represent the force that allows everything to "be" what it is and to continue "being." These angels represent the connection and the continuity between Source and the unfolding creation.

This conception of angels includes the entire universe. We will engage this view in considerable depth when we later encounter the angels Metatron, Sandalphon, and the Shekhina in Part Four. On the more individual level, the main encounters we have are with archangels and guardian angels. Keep in mind, however, that the story of Balaam gives us pause to consider the possibility that as we sit or stand right now, we are surrounded by many angelic forms.

The donkey that we ride is viewed by some as this body of ours; I prefer to view it as our own minds. The mind carries us to wherever we go. It is a faithful servant when well handled. The mind also can be a stubborn ass; it can and often does insist on going its own way. Sometimes it won't go at all. This is what happens when we abuse our own minds. But the mind can be trained, and it can serve us well. There are many tools to work with in this training. One of the primary tools is that of cultivation. The mind can be cultivated like a beautiful field. It may simply take some effort to plow in order to open up fixated or constricted thinking.

As mentioned earlier, the method of cultivation as a contemplative practice is to use imagination to enter states of mind that help shift our moods and perspectives. Through the use of memory, for example, we can simulate events that made us happy, joyful, calm, loving, and so forth, feelings that induce a change in our thoughts and behavior. Through recognition and repetition we can condition ourselves to various mood states at will. In so doing, we can actually alter the way we respond to certain events, building openness and skillfulness in our own behavior.

As we will now see, the archangels can be identified with specific characteristics. By learning their stories and by associating certain traits with individual angels, we can begin to use the powers of our own imagination to bring ourselves in closer alignment with their characteristics. This kind of practice, which is done in many traditions, can be quite transformative—as we will now explore.

THE ARCHANGEL MICHAEL

The name *Michael* in Hebrew literally means "who is like God (El)." The archangel Michael (pronounced in Hebrew "Meh-khi-ayl") is envisioned as "standing" to the right of the throne of God, and indeed, this angel is considered in many ways to be the right hand of God.

In kabbalistic terms, the right hand of God represents mercy and lovingkindness. This association appears many times in normative Jewish practice. A *mezuzah* is put on the right side of the entrance door to one's home; traditional practitioners put a mezuzah on the right side of every doorway in the home. Traditional Jews put their right shoe on before their left. They light a right candle before a left one; they hold the *Kiddush* wine cup in the right hand. Blessings of children are usually done with the right hand. The Torah makes references to the right thigh (for taking an oath), the right ear, and the right thumb for certain rituals.

In each of these acts and many others, one can invite the sense of mercy, lovingkindness, openheartedness, and caring. By simply thinking about what one is doing in a way that evokes in oneself feelings of mercy and lovingkindness, one can shift one's mood and sensitivity in this direction. When we do this, we are imagining a sense of presence that we can actually feel. We are softened in this process, becoming more relaxed and more open.

Most of us have the experience of occasionally sensing something by our side or nearby in the room. The sensation usually arises spontaneously, and it can have a particular emotion attached to it. Often, when we look to see, we find nothing. Then we usually ignore the experience and write it off to a trick of the mind, but at other times it is so strong we cannot deny the feeling that something is there.

Sometimes there actually *is* someone there, or there is a knowing of something about to happen that proves to be correct. When this intuitive knowing proves to be true, we assume that such experiences are either subtle cues that are subconscious or that perhaps there is a touch of Grace from an unknown source. Many of us have had a taste of such experiences. However, mystical practitioners teach that we do not have to wait for the finger of Grace to alert us to these moments; rather, we can practice invoking certain experiences and feelings in a way that sensitizes us and makes us more available.

We can begin by cultivating the experience of being at ease and at peace. This usually leads to a feeling of openheartedness. When such a feeling happens, we can associate it with the name Michael. At first this is an "artificial" association. However, by training ourselves through repetition, an association can be created in a short time so that all we need do is think of the name

Michael, and our mood rapidly shifts. (Be sure to keep the association with the Archangel Michael, a vision we will develop, rather than to any human Michael you may know.) The experience of this archangel is *not* like having someone else in the room; it is the experience that would be expressed by saying, "I am feeling open and loving right now."

One might ask, why bother making such an association? Why not simply imagine lovingkindness all the time and let it affect our mood until we become better people? The answer is quite simply that as much as most people *want* to be openhearted, we are almost all lost in our own narrow view of the world. Most of us need "tools" to help us develop our spiritual potential, and this is what contemplative practice is all about.

The point is not that someone must "believe" in angels to embrace the potential empowerment of dwelling in certain mind states. Just as there are well-known positive effects in medicine and psychology that can be stimulated through the use of the imagination, so too are there opportunities for invoking our own hidden potential by taking on practices that strengthen our attitudes, moods, convictions, and other powerful states of mind. The idea of angels, particularly archangels, is embedded in our collective unconscious, and this adds strength on a primordial level to our practice. We should not underestimate these powers hidden within our own psyches.

As previously mentioned, the archangel Michael is mostly associated with acts of lovingkindness. We see in the Torah that one of Michael's tasks was to inform Abraham and Sarah of the upcoming birth of their son Isaac. This birth was considered a miracle as both parents were both quite advanced in age—Abraham being one hundred years old and Sarah ninety (Gen. 17:17).

In the oral tradition, Michael was the angel that accompanied Eliezer, Abraham's servant, in the search for Isaac's soulmate. Michael and Gabriel both witnessed the sale of Esau's birthright to Jacob; they both were present when the Torah was given to Moses.

We do occasionally find Michael in a fierce role. Michael is viewed as one of the angels who caused the destruction of Sennacherib, the king of Assyria and Babylonia in the seventh century BCE. As tradition tells the story, on the first night of Passover the angel Michael went forth and destroyed the entire Assyrian army of 185,000 soldiers. Some historians say it was actually a plague that struck the army; from my perspective both viewpoints are completely compatible—all so-called "acts of God" are carried out by angels.

The specific visualization work we will do with the energy of Michael is to reflect upon moments of unusual openheartedness that we have experienced. We reflect upon periods of great generosity, sharing, caring, and being available. The reflections can be of our own acts of lovingkindness or those of others. We repeat these images over and over again. We will do this on the next track of the CD.

We then allow ourselves to remember situations in which there may not have been much lovingkindness where we held back, feeling tightfisted and contracted. We allow ourselves to recall these situations and feel the tightness in our hearts.

Then, using our imaginations, we allow ourselves to "pretend" that we are able to remember an event in an entirely new way, this time with a completely open heart and a generous spirit. This wishful thinking that we bring to the situation has a quality of softening our hearts. Our intention is not to feel remorseful about our past deeds; rather it is to reflect and recommit ourselves to becoming more generous of heart from this time forward. By imagining ourselves engaged in situations in a new way, we begin to build our potential for automatically bringing greater openheartedness to new situations that arise.

This is our practice in the name of Michael. We will have a different practice for each of the major archangels. As we do the long version of the Archangel Meditation, our visualizations will become richer, allowing us to deepen our connection with each of the selected angels. The audio recording you are about to hear is a longer version of the initial meditation we did on the first track of the CD. In this upcoming version, we distinguish in detail the attributes associated with each of the key archangels. Listening to this longer track repeatedly, we absorb on a visceral level the identity of each angel. In so doing, we develop immediate recognition of the feelings associated with the archangels so that when we repeat the shorter version, which takes less than a minute, we can quickly invoke the energy of the appropriate archangel for any particular situation.

Each time an archangel is described in writing, you will be asked once again to review the long version of the Archangel Meditation. Doing each of these repetitions when they are suggested will allow you to master this particular meditative experience.

LISTEN TO TRACK 4
Archangel Meditation
(long form)

While working with the archangel Michael at the beginning of this meditation, let yourself reflect on a time of great gratitude when you felt the blessings of compassion and openheartedness, either in yourself or in someone else. Immerse yourself in these feelings, and allow your thinking mind to rest, inviting a calm state to soothe and quiet your soul.

THE ARCHANGEL GABRIEL

The word Gabriel (pronounced Gav-ree-ayl in Hebrew) means "the justice or righteousness of God." The root form of the word, g-v-r, is connected with courage and heroism, as well as the word for "man." Thus, Gabriel could be literally translated as "man of God," one who courageously lives according to the universal laws. The root of Gabriel is also connected with the attribute of Gevorah, which, in kabbalistic terminology, is seen as the left side of God. Whereas Michael is on God's right hand, Gabriel is on God's left hand. The left hand is the one that metes out punishment; the right hand overrules strict justice and is more lenient.

Gabriel is the angel that is sent to destroy the cities of sin, Sodom and Gomorrah. Some sources say that it was Gabriel—not Michael—that annihilated Sennacherib's camp. This view is obviously more consistent with the general description of these two archangels; however, it is important to note that biblical commentaries are often in opposition to one another, depending upon the point being made. The realms of souls, angels, and heavenly beings are beyond definitive description—they are trans-rational. Therefore, we must be careful not to assign intellectual constructs when discussing them. Still, we can probe the depths of our own beings to find ways to connect with parts of ourselves that are amenable to self-empowerment, each of which can be associated with one or more angels.

It is taught that Gabriel is in charge of souls and also in charge of the Moon. The Moon, in Kabbalah, is considered to be the dwelling place of souls that have not yet been bound to physical bodies. Gabriel is also viewed as one of the main assistants of the Angel of Death, who will be discussed in the final part of this book.

As noted, biblical commentators often contradict one another in various stories where an unnamed angel appears, particularly in the case of Gabriel or Michael. There is general agreement, nonetheless, that when either of these angels is experienced, the Divine is present. When these particular angels are doing their job, so to speak, they remove some veils of confusion to reveal the Divine Presence. This can be seen in a number of episodes in the Bible.

An example would be in Genesis 18, in the exchange between Abraham and the angels who informed him of the birth of Isaac. This same section includes an encounter between Abraham and God, plus an added interaction regarding the destruction of Sodom. In these instances, we are not certain which angel is being represented. This is how it appears in the Bible:

"It [the angel Michael or Gabriel] said [to Abraham], '*I will return* next year; and, behold, Sarah your wife shall have a son.' [When Sarah heard this] she laughed, and asked herself, 'Even though I am old and [Abraham] is also old, will I have this joy?'" (Gen. 18:12) Immediately following this, there is a shift of subject: "*And the Lord asked Abraham* [directly], 'Why did Sarah laugh? Is any thing too hard for the Lord? At the time appointed *I will return to you,* at this season, and Sarah shall have a son ...'"

The Bible now continues: "And the Lord said [directly, to Abraham], 'Because the cry of Sodom and Gomorrah is great and because their sin is very grave; *I will go down now, and see what they have done.' And the men* [angels] *turned away and went toward Sodom; but Abraham still stood before the Lord*" (Gen. 18:22).

Another example in which we are not certain of the angel's identity is the story of Moses and the burning bush. In the oral tradition, some say this angel was Michael, some say Gabriel, some say Zagzagael; it is almost certain that others have been identified. (Interestingly, oral tradition describes these three angels as the ones who attended Moses at the time of his death.)

Regarding the burning bush, the Torah teaches:

"The angel of the Lord appeared to him in a flame of fire from the middle of a bush. [Moses] looked and the bush burned with fire, but was not consumed. Moses said to himself, 'I will stop, look and see this great sight—why the bush is not burnt.' When the Lord saw that [Moses] had stopped and turned, God called to him out of the midst of the bush, and said, 'Moses, Moses.' And he [Moses] said, 'Here am I'" (Ex. 3:3).

The oral tradition expresses wonder that a thorn bush was at the center of this exchange, and says that one reason is to teach that God's Presence can be found in the lowliest forms of creation—including a seemingly meaningless bush in the middle of the desert.

The important point to note here is that the commentators of the oral tradition use the biblical stories as wisdom teachings, and they make free use of the tools of biblical analysis to make their points. The angels have characteristics associated with their names. When the angel Zagzagael is invoked, it means literally "zagzag," to polish or make transparent, and "El," a name of God. So using Zagzagael as the angel suggests the idea of "making something transparent so that God can be seen." In this way, the angel of the burning bush represents something like the looking glass of *Alice in Wonderland*, a mystical gateway for seeing into extraordinary realms.

When associated with the archangel Michael, the burning bush becomes a story connected with the attribute of merciful lovingkindness. When associated with the archangel Gabriel, the burning bush is connected with justice and law. As the story unfolds and God speaks to Moses, any of the above points can be demonstrated.

If the emphasis of the burning bush story is that God is revealed to Moses through the fire, then we would assume that the name of the angel was

Zagzagael, whose name represents the transparency through which God can be seen. If, on the other hand, the message of this story is focused on ending the affliction of the Israelites through acts of mercy and lovingkindness, then the angel associated would be Michael. If the ending of the Israelites' affliction will come through justice and strong discipline, then the angel associated would be Gabriel. Depending upon the teaching that one derives from biblical stories, the names used to represent God—or the names of various angels who represent divine attributes—are key factors in how a reading is to be understood.

The archangels Michael and Gabriel represent two opposite poles. They are both viewed as princes—meaning they each represent clear archetypes— and there are distinct differences in the qualities of each. When we see, for example, a driver speeding recklessly and dangerously but surviving without being stopped by the police or causing an accident, we feel the presence of Michael. When we see someone getting a speeding ticket or worse, a terrible wreck on the side of the road, we experience the presence of Gabriel. We encounter dozens of events like this every day. The way we react reveals the *angel-field* of consciousness at that moment.

This idea of an angel-field is the psychospiritual way of working with angels. It is a way for us to participate as co-creators in the unfolding of creation, rather than being passive observers as angel entities are assumed to come and go on their own.

We all know firsthand that various events in life evoke feelings within each of us. These feelings, however subtle, are always connected with the angelic realms—that is to say, we are never separate from our own sensations, our own emotions, our own thoughts, and our own inner urges that pull us toward raising our consciousness (our "good" inclination), or in the direction of letting go into lower levels of consciousness (our "not-good" inclination).

Thus, we can notice an open and expansive mood or a contracted, tight mood. We can move from one to the other, depending upon our inner focus, without much of a change in what is happening around us. If we cling to these moods, our activities will be influenced by them; if we hold them lightly, and witness them with a slight detachment (which is what angel consciousness invokes), our activities will not be as dependent upon our changing moods.

Play Track 4 once again. This time work carefully with the description and imagination of Gabriel. Feel the power of your connection with your true nature. Allow yourself to recognize the interconnectedness of all things—how small actions can have major implications, both for good and not-so-good. Let yourself know that you are responsible for the way your world unfolds, and feel the strength of your commitment and your own abilities.

LISTEN TO TRACK 4
Archangel Meditation
(long form)

THE ARCHANGEL RAPHAEL

The archangel Raphael is the angel dedicated to healing. In addition to the healing of humans, this angel is charged with healing the earth and all of its creatures. Raphael is also the angel that defended God's decision to create humans against the wishes of almost all of the other angels, who believed that it was a grave mistake to create such an offensive, troublemaking, and mostly unconscious species. The jury is still out.

In the Bible, Moses's sister, Miriam, criticizes Moses on his behavior and is punished by God. The punishment is that she is afflicted with a type of leprosy (Num. 12). Moses is distraught and prays, "God, please heal her now."

In Hebrew, Moses' prayer reads, *El nah refah nah lah,* and this is the source of this angel's name: *Rafah-El.*

In Jewish mythology, the gift of wisdom was given to primordial humans metaphorically as a book called the Book of Adam. This book was initially given to Adam by the angel Raziel, whose name means "the secrets of God." In many ways, the wisdom contained in this book is what defines and distinguishes human consciousness and its full potential. Without this wisdom, humans are no better nor more gifted than other animal life. The unique potential of human wisdom—when raised to its highest level—is that it can reveal the true nature of the meaning and purpose of life.

As the story goes, Adam (and Eve) ate the fruit of the Tree of Knowledge of Good and Evil, misguided by the serpent (the master of confusion) who promised that this fruit would give them the wisdom they sought. Instead, the opposite happened: the instant the fruit was tasted, the Book of Adam disappeared, leaving our primordial parents in an illusory state of mind, a mind that misconstrues the true nature of things—which is just how our minds continue to work today. When Adam realized what was lost, he wept copiously and immersed himself up to his neck in the river Gihon—one of the four mystical streams emanating from the Garden of Eden—symbolizing that he was no longer able to deal with the Garden and all that it provided if he could not have access to the true meaning of his existence.

Thus it is taught that in Adam's grief God signaled to Raphael to return the book, which Adam then studied for the rest of his life. The book was inherited by Adam's son Seth, and it went through the early generations to Abraham, who taught the world about the true nature of Oneness. Still, only a handful of humans throughout all these years have been privileged to understand the full truth of the teaching of Oneness.

We learn from these stories that Raphael is the angel we invoke when we ourselves are not well, physically or mentally; when our beloved friends or family are suffering; or when we are praying for the end to suffering of all beings and for the end of suffering of nature and Mother Earth.

It is interesting to note that each of the four primary archangels is connected with a symbolic creature, described by the prophet Ezekiel in a vision—considered to be one of the most significant mystical revelations in the entire scripture. In this vision, Michael appears with the face of a lion, Gabriel with the face of an Ox, Uriel—whom we will discuss in the next section—with the face of an eagle, and Raphael with the face of a man. Of all the angels and archangels, Raphael is in many ways the "friendliest," most accommodating intermediary between humans and the great multitudes of angels in the various realms.

Raphael is envisioned as standing directly in back of us, supporting us at all times. Moving behind us, Raphael cleans up our mistakes and erases any disturbances we may have left behind on our path. Raphael is the one who tidies up so that we do not leave too much evidence of our passage through life or cause too much harm through ill-spoken words or unskillful actions.

Please play Track 4 again, this time focused on Raphael, keeping in mind that the angel's name is derived from the Hebrew prayer in which Moses called out to God: *Ana El nah refah nah lah* (Please, God, heal her now). Let yourself imagine a time when you needed healing for yourself or a beloved. Remember how it feels to call out for help, and allow yourself to rest back into the arms of this healing energy that is always just behind you.

LISTEN TO TRACK 4
Archangel Meditation
(long form)

THE ARCHANGEL URIEL

The archangel Uriel, whose name means "light of God," was the messenger sent to Noah to announce the coming of the Flood. As the story of the Flood captured the imagination of many commentators, there is a fairly wide array of angels mentioned. Some say it was Raziel—the angel connected with Adam and the mysterious book—who appeared to Noah so that he would have instructions on how to build the ark.

The late professor Gershom Scholem of Hebrew University, who popularized the study of Kabbalah a half-century ago, said that Raziel and Uriel were one and the same. Indeed, from a mystical perspective, they have identical numeric values. The Hebrew letters of each of their names add up to 248, which is a kabbalistic proof that there must be a distinct relationship between these two. Another way of saying this is that the revelation of "secrets" (Raziel) brings a special "light" (Uriel) that raises one's awareness of the nature of Presence.

Some say it was Raphael who originally gave Adam the book; others say Raphael gave Noah a different book at the end of the Flood, a book on medicine and healing. Some say angels actually assisted Noah in the building of the ark.

In Judaism, the Torah is examined word by word, letter by letter, in the belief that as a holy document it contains all of the secrets of creation. In this process, the sages have analyzed virtually every textual difficulty and all apparent inconsistencies in an attempt to reveal hidden divine teachings. There are many mystical explanations for problems that cannot be solved rationally. This is why we find angels everywhere throughout the oral tradition.

Consider the story of Noah as an example. The commentators were certainly troubled by how Noah knew to design the Ark to survive the Flood, how to build such an ark, why it had the specific design elements described in the Torah, and how Noah knew the way to prepare for a lengthy period of survival. Thousands of questions have arisen on issues as obvious as how Noah kept predatory animals alongside their prey—lions and lambs living together in peace while on the ark.

As we dig more deeply into these kinds of commentaries, we discover interesting hints about the qualities being probed. Regarding the archangel Uriel, the light of God, we find in kabbalistic literature that when Noah was instructed by an angel on the building of the ark, he engraved the teachings in a mystical precious stone, a sapphire, which he then built into the ark as a kind of skylight. This stone was a mystical source of light and became the main source of illumination for the ark.

The oral tradition teaches that during the entire twelve months of the Flood, Noah did not need normal daylight or moonlight, for the engraved sapphire of illumination shone all the time. The Hebrew word for sapphire is *sappir,* which has the same root connected with the word *sefirah,* which represents the emanation, or radiance, of God. While the sages argued over the true meaning of this divine illumination, it is quite clear from a kabbalistic perspective that this illumination symbolizes the continuous presence of the angel Uriel.

There are many descriptions in various traditions of a powerful light that glows when one is experiencing a high level of consciousness. This is Uriel, the archangel who rules over all the luminaries of the heavens. Its light is so penetrating that Uriel is the primary guide one can use to navigate through the darkest places of our minds. Indeed, one of Uriel's primary tasks is to guide an army of angels into the depths of the netherworld.

When forgiveness reigns, Uriel carries the light of mercy. However, there are different kinds of light. Occasionally, a light of God is represented by an angel named Nuriel. This kind of light is quite different from that of Uriel, for it represents the harsh severity of justice and payment in kind for one's misdeeds—it is a light that has little room for forgiveness.

Uriel, then, is the angel we wish to evoke when we have been carried into a darkness or despair that requires a special light—an all-encompassing light of mercy and wisdom that will guide us out. We must be aware, however, that Uriel also represents a light of illuminated truth, which means we must be prepared to see and recognize aspects of ourselves and of the situation that have caused this darkness.

Uriel is connected with the special light that glows within all beings, a light so clear and so bright that we can see it right in front of our faces even in total daylight. Most commentators agree that Uriel stands directly in front of the Throne of God and therefore should be envisioned as a light in front of us that we are continually entering.

Please play Track 4 once again, focusing on Uriel's characteristics. As you listen to the description of Uriel, allow yourself to close your eyes and imag-

LISTEN TO TRACK 4
Archangel Meditation
(long form)

ine a light glowing brighter and brighter in front of you and within you. Let this powerful light penetrate and fill your body with the glow of divine radiance. This is a wonderful experience and will prove extraordinarily useful when you are in difficult, crowded, or threatening situations in which you need help generating the light of wisdom and compassion. ✦

PART FOUR

The Supreme Angels

METATRON

Metatron, the *sar ha-panim,* or prince of the Presence, is the greatest, largest, most important of all angels, second only to the Presence itself and some-times even confused with the YHVH, the Source of Being. Some Jewish mystics refer to the sar ha-panim as the "little YHVH," which is only one step under God, so to speak. An earlier name for this angel was Yahoel, which translates as either the "breath of God" or the "God-face presence of God." In other words, this angel is in many ways a greater presence than all of the archangels combined.

In traditional Judaism, even to this day, one is hesitant to say the name of this angel out loud or even to write it. This is why I will refer to this supreme angel as M throughout this chapter. In kabbalistic circles, this angel is often referred to as "the youth," "the lad," or "the boy," as a typical, intentional understatement that is often used by the sages to say just the opposite of what they mean—in this instance, "the enormous," "the beyond measure," or "the gigantic."

In the Talmud, a sage once considered the possibility that there were perhaps "two powers," suggesting two deities, which of course is heresy in Judaism. This sage was quickly disabused of these dualistic thoughts. He was given a vision of M being struck with sixty blows of red-hot rods as a demonstration that this was an angel—not a god. Despite M's enormity—as large as the universe—it could still be made humble and therefore was not a god.

It is thought that M's name may have been derived from a combination of the Greek *meta* and *thronos,* meaning "one who serves behind the throne." This suggests that M is the hidden true power behind creation and everything that unfolds in the universe. Most scholars agree, however, that the source of the name is more likely to be the word *metator,* which means "guide." In fact, some say that the cloud and fire that guided the Israelites when they first escaped to the wilderness was actually the angel M.

This idea of the Spirit of Guidance as a universal force is the subject of a beautiful Sufi invocation that reads:

> Toward the One, the Perfection of Love, Harmony and Beauty, the Only Being, United with all the Illuminated Souls who form the embodiment of the Master, The Spirit of Guidance.

This invocation could be M's mantra.

When we seriously practice any authentic spiritual exercise, we sooner or later come to the recognition that we are not individuals seeking some exalted goal for ourselves, but are sparks of Oneness, the Only Being, aspects of the total embodiment of the Spirit of Guidance that leads all of creation back to the Source, the perfection of love, harmony, and beauty. In our motivation to attain the highest levels of awareness, we eventually release our personal identification and become completely connected with an inner guide, a metamagnetic urge that prods us at all times to let go into the Oneness.

M is associated in the Bible with Enoch, father of Methuselah. Enoch is one of two biblical characters who tradition teaches never died—the other being Elijah. The language of the Bible says that "Enoch walked with God, and he disappeared [was "nothing"] for God took him" (Ex. 5:24). Many sages argued that everyone has to die, despite the power of miracles, so Enoch could not live forever. One solution was to suggest that rather than being a human who became an angel, M was always an angel who temporarily took the form of a human in the guise of Enoch. This sidesteps the issue of a creature who never dies, for as an angel, Enoch was never born as a human. However we choose to interpret the biblical language, it is generally agreed by commentators that there is a definite association between Enoch and the supreme angel M.

As an apparent human, Enoch was the keeper in his time of the Book of Adam. It is said that he foresaw what would be on the tablets that were later given to Moses on the mountain. He also possessed the miraculous rod that Moses would use when confronting the Pharaoh. He knew the secrets of the heavens and celebrated special calendar days long before they were revealed to Moses in the Torah. While on earth, he remained hidden except when instructed to teach others—and his teachings were said to cause peace on earth during the period he taught. He lived in human form for 365 years.

As an angel, M ascended to the heavens in a glowing chariot of fire, pulled by horses of flame. In the heavenly realms, all the supernal mysteries beyond those given in the Torah were revealed to him, and he was shown the Garden of Eden with the Tree of Knowledge. This is all described in another mysterious book of wisdom, the Book of Enoch, which has had enormous influence over many centuries for those who study the mysteries of the cosmos.

The numerical value of the Hebrew letters that make up the name of M is 314, which is identical with the numerical value of the God-name *Shaddai.* Shaddai comes from the root that means "breast," thus Shaddai is often referred to as the "breasted God." Its features are strength, protection, and nurturing, which is why containers for mezuzahs that are on the doorposts of many Jewish homes are marked with the Hebrew letter *shin,* symbolizing the first letter of the God-name Shaddai.

There is another interpretation of Shaddai, which comes from *sha,* which means "who," and *dai,* which means "enough." This combination then could mean "who is enough." In the classic kabbalistic text, the Zohar, the word "who" is yet another name of God, so this phrase "who is enough" is not treated as a question, but as an assertion: "Who (God) is enough!" In this context, Shaddai is essentially the idea of sufficiency.

Whether at the breast of the omnipotent mother or in the arms of omniscient knowledge, wherever we are, right now, this moment is filled with God and therefore is enough just as it is. This is a powerful idea that suggests we can constantly rest in the power and the recognition of the sufficiency of this moment; M's main attribute is connected with this everlasting sufficiency.

From all that we have learned above about M and other angels, we can more clearly experience the sparkling imagery of the symbolism connected with Kabbalah and the names given angels. One who reads mystical texts without a background in the derivation of these names misses an enormous amount of deeper meanings hidden in the texts. Knowing these hidden teachings and learning how to visualize them opens new gateways that can empower us in the characteristics we are studying in this book: mercy, judgment, wisdom, healing, and the Divine Presence.

As an example, read with new eyes an excerpt from the Zohar:

> Sixty mighty beings surround the king [Ein Sof] representing sixty rods of judgment [Gabriel] that gird the youth [M], who holds a flashing sword in the right hand [Michael] and coals of fire with seventy thousand consuming flames in the left [Gabriel] ... All the beings gather at midnight [Gevorah/Gabriel] and the youth [M] who sucks at his mother's [Shekhina's] breasts [Shaddai] purify them.... Midnight [Gevorah/Gabriel] is a special time of unity [Shekhina] when all come together under the wings [Chesed/Michael] of the Source [Ein Sof], and all experience both its wisdom [Uriel] and its mercy [Michael].

Finally, regarding the mystical perspective of M, we find that the Zohar distinguishes between the idea of an "Academy of Heaven" and an "Academy on High." The Academy of Heaven is overseen by M, while the Academy on High is directly managed by the Source Itself. There are other "lower" academies, such as the Academy of Moses and the Academy of Aaron. In this context, we see once again that M is only one step below the Godhead. In a way, as Ein Sof is never accessible or imaginable, anything we can imagine as the ultimate power of the universe must, by definition, be in the realm of the supreme angel, M. Even the messiah is viewed as being in M's academy.

As you listen to the next audio track, try to keep in mind that there is a force that enlivens us and everything around us. It is not only the spark of life; it is "the mover" beneath everything that exists, the sustainer of all motion, the continuity that holds everything together. It is moving you at this moment, in every moment. Everything you experience is motivated by this force. If it withdrew itself even for an instant, the entire universe would immediately vanish. Moreover, it provides us with everything we need in order to be who we are, what we are, and where we are at all times and in all ways.

LISTEN TO TRACK 5
Meditation on Metatron

SANDALPHON

Sandalphon is viewed as M's lesser brother, yet is so awesome that he, too, is supreme, ruling legions of angels and the highest (seventh) level of the heavens. These brother angels tend to all prayers: Sandalphon weaves them into a mystical crown for the "head" of God, and M handles the response to the petitioner, the one who prays. Sandalphon represents all matter and form of the universe (the *yesh*, or "thingness" aspect of Ein Sof), while M represents the essential emptiness out of which everything arises and into which everything disappears (the *ayin*, or "nothingness" aspect of Ein Sof).

Sandalphon is in many ways the primary intermediary between heaven and earth, between emptiness and form, between source and creation. Kabbalists say that the derivation of Sandalphon's name is composed of two parts: *sandal*, a stillborn embryo not yet distinguishable, and *fon*, the root of the word "face," which together mean "matter in the process of becoming a face/form."

Sandalphon does not have the same power as M, but he still causes the angels and all the hosts of other realms to quiver in awe. It is said that Sandalphon is so large it would take five hundred years to traverse his entire body, which is the Talmudic way of saying that Sandalphon is at least as big as our entire universe.

This angel takes all prayers every day and, as mentioned, weaves them into a gigantic crown. He then utters a charm, a secret name of God, magically sending the crown beyond all limits of this universe, which causes all the hosts of all the realms to be so astonished that they tremble, shake, and sing out: *Holy! Holy! Holy! is the Lord of Hosts, the whole earth is filled with its glory!*

As the crown reaches the Throne of God beyond all universes, the "foundation" and "wheels" of the throne begin shaking, and every part of the universe vibrates. Every aspect of creation "speaks out" in universal harmony, praising creation and the life that goes with it.

From a kabbalistic perspective, this process is continuously occurring and is the source that sustains the unending motion of every bit of matter in the universe. In modern terms, this is connected with string theory. In physics, nothing exists at absolute zero, which is the hypothetical point at which all movement stops. We see here that prayer is a crucial element in sustaining the universe, and Sandalphon is the medium through which prayer is communicated from "below" to "above."

We should note that prayer takes many forms. Human words of prayer that we construct in our minds make up only a tiny percentage of the vast array of prayer. A mother's groans in childbirth are a special form of prayer; a cry of grief is prayer; a loving glance is prayer. On the nonhuman level, all life prays in its own way continuously. Nothing lives without prayer; everything constantly communicates with the Source of Life. A breath is a prayer, hunger is a prayer, the taste of nourishment is a prayer, and that which nourishes prays in its own way. Even a heartbeat is a prayer. All of this comes under the purview of Sandalphon.

Sandalphon and M each assumed a human form for a period of time—M as Enoch and Sandalphon as Elijah (Eliyahu). Each left the human realm in a chariot of fire drawn by steeds of flame. In this sense, each is viewed as being eternal.

The main difference between Enoch and Elijah is that Enoch disappears completely into the heavenly realms, while Elijah often reappears in a human form and will continue to do so until he completes his task of announcing the transformation of human consciousness into messianic consciousness. In biblical language this appears in the prophesy of Malachi (Mal. 3:23), who says that Elijah will appear just before a "great and terrible day" to "turn the hearts" of parent to child and child to parent, which will mark the coming of a new messianic age.

Whereas Sandalphon in angelic form is not widely recognized, Elijah as a prophet and as the herald of the Messiah is very well known in Western tradition—popularized in Christianity and Islam as well as in Judaism. Jewish sages concluded that Elijah remains the key angelic force for resolving disputes and is considered to be the paradigm of the greatest potential for peacemaking in the world.

There are hundreds of stories describing Elijah's appearances on earth in various guises. His name appears dozens of times in the Bible, close to one hundred times in the Zohar, and over three hundred times in the Talmud. The number of Hasidic tales that mention Elijah runs well into thousands. Elijah is regularly invoked in Jewish prayers, is called upon at the end of every Sabbath, and is invited to the dinner table at a key moment at every Passover Seder.

Elijah's primary attributes have to do with conflict resolution and helping people who are in difficulty—the poor, the homeless, and the elderly. In the story of Esther, Elijah is an invisible force that trips up Haman, who is driven to destroy the Jewish population. Elijah is constantly battling with the Dark Side. This supreme angel is perhaps best known as a fighter for political, social, and economic justice. He is the Robin Hood of angels, taking from the rich and giving to the poor.

Elijah is often portrayed as a beggar in rags, a stranger in need, or a simpleton with unusual wisdom. He often punishes those who are unjust or works miracles for those in need. He is also one to turn to for problems of infertility. He is the guardian angel for newborn children for the first thirty days, and, indeed, at every traditional Jewish circumcision, which normally takes place on the eighth day after birth, a special Chair of Elijah is used for the person holding the infant during the actual ceremony.

Elijah is also well known for bringing the dead to life, a specific example of which is described in the Bible (1Kings: 17). For this reason, Elijah is seen as the primary opponent of the Angel of Death, who will be discussed in Part Five.

When doing the meditation on Track 6 on the supreme angel Sandalphon, you are invited to imagine the experience of being immersed in a sea of light. Every part of the body is illuminated by everything that touches it, by everything it sees and hears, and by everything that moves in the universe. This state of mind is a surrendering, a merging, a letting go of the separate self. In this state, everything is energized by a divine spark, and in this sense all is connected to the Source.

LISTEN TO TRACK 6
Meditation on Sandalphon

THE SHEKHINA

The word *shechane* in Hebrew means "a neighbor or an inhabitant of a place," and *Shekhina* has the special meaning of being the Divine Presence. The "ah" sound at the end of a word in Hebrew usually indicates the feminine gender. Thus, the Shekhina is viewed in traditional Judaism as God's Divine Presence, which is a feminine aspect. In addition, the same root is found in the word *Mishkan,* which in times past was the home of the Shekhina. In the Hebrew Bible, the Mishkan was considered to be the dwelling place of God on Earth, a portable sanctuary that was carried by the Hebrews during their years of wandering in the desert.

What is meant by Divine Presence? In the earliest times, the Presence was seen as beyond something most people could face. If the high priest of the Temple of Jerusalem entered the Holy of Holies—a special chamber in the center of the Temple— and stood in the physical presence of God, a single ill-timed thought of the priest would result in his immediate death. On Yom Kippur day, when the high priest was obliged to enter the Holy of Holies and speak the secret name, a rope was tied around the priest's waist so that if he died because of his wandering thoughts, those standing on the outside would be able to pull him out. Otherwise, whoever attempted to retrieve the dead priest would himself surely risk death by his own impure thoughts.

The ancient idea of God as a being with substance changed long ago. There was a shift in consciousness toward a more abstract notion of God. God was not viewed as dwelling in the Holy of Holies, but was everywhere—shapeless, without form. This sense of the abstract nature of God is given sharp definition in the book of Deuteronomy, the final book of the Five Books of Moses, which shifts the emphasis from the corporeal form of God that appears in the first four books and begins to refer to God as "The Name." This beginning of a "name theology" is the reason the ancient rabbis were very careful to avoid pronouncing specific names of God, because a given name implies a form to which the name is connected.

The abstract notion of God gained more significance through kabbalistic insights. Kabbalists all along said that the Ein Sof, the boundless Source of Life, was indescribable. There were no attributes that could be designated, there was nothing to label; in every way Boundlessness is nothingness and everythingness simultaneously. Moreover, the universe we observe that is full of life and movement must be an expression of the Divine—what else could it be? But this universe does not set limits on Boundlessness.

In the Zohar, one of the most important source books of Kabbalah, this expression of Boundlessness is called the Matrona, the Great Mother, also known as the Shekhina, the primordial Feminine Presence. In mystical imagery, this Presence is viewed not only as mother, but as sister, daughter, and the most intimate beloved of the Source.

The Shekhina is not considered as separate from Boundlessness, nor can it be separated from anything that happens in the universe. The Shekhina has been described by the scholar J. Abelson as "a world-permeating force, a reality in the world of matter or mind, the immanent aspect of God, holding all things under its omnipresent sway."

The essential point of Kabbalah is that the nature of the Source is an unending vital flow that sustains every movement in the universe—with the crucial understanding that this ongoing flow is not only outward into Creation, as if it were separate, but into Itself, for God is *not* separate from anything. The Source is paradoxically the immutable, unchangeable, dynamically flowing Now!

The instrument of all change and all matter that exists is the Shekhina. Moreover, not only is the Shekhina viewed as the Great Mother of this universe, it is also seen as the Great Mother of all worlds, including the realms of the angels and demons.

The Shekhina gained this all-inclusive stature in Judaism mainly in the twelfth and thirteenth centuries, when Kabbalah came into its fullness and the Zohar was first published. The Zohar has over seven hundred references to the Shekhina, such as:

> It is incumbent on a person ... that the Shekhina may never depart. ... By offering prayers and thanksgiving, the person brings the Shekhina to rest within ... through this union with the Shekhina, the person becomes balanced and unified.... At all times, the person should be very careful of his or her actions, so that this celestial partner will stay within.... When one gives joy to the Shekhina, it spreads peace in the world (Zohar 1:50a).

This idea of merging with the Shekhina is an elementary kabbalistic teaching. It is the goal of all Jewish mystics to enter into a state of *devekut*, being "at one" with the Divine, living in the Presence at all times. While the language of the Zohar is often erotic, like the images described in the highly mystical Song of Songs, the intention is to transcend ordinary sexuality and attain a spiritual coherence in which one becomes indivisible from the Source of Life.

As the Great Mother, the Shekhina births all that participates in creation. It represents the emptiness out of which everything arises and into which everything disappears. It represents the form of everything that takes shape as matter as well as the potential for life.

The meditation on the Shekhina appears as the final track on the accompanying CD. This is an extraordinary meditation that builds upon the two supreme angels M and Sandalphon, who represent, respectively, the nothingness out of which everything arises and the everythingness that is included in the totality of the universe.

This closing meditation is best experienced if you imagine yourself completely embraced in the arms of the Great Mother: totally secure, at ease, as safe and at as much peace as possible. Nothing at all is needed. In these tender but strong arms we are loved, we are nurtured, we are protected, and we are free. This is the experience of being fully merged with the Presence, without any concerns about the past or worries about the future. This is what the Shekhina is about. ◈

LISTEN TO TRACK 7
Meditation on the Shekhina

PART FIVE

The Fallen Angels

DEMONIC FORCES

Angelic forces are regularly at odds with demonic forces. While our emphasis in this book is on invoking "good" angels, it is important to understand the character of the Other Side as well. Traditionally, and in order to avoid suggesting that there was a purposeful creation of demons, the ancient scholars developed a mythology around angels who failed their calling for one reason or another—fallen angels. We need to be clear, however, that even the idea of angels falling away from the God-field and becoming separate entities in conflict with the will of God is completely unacceptable in monotheistic theology.

Instead, we are taught in Hasidism that each and every aspect of creation is empowered by a divine spark, which is naturally perfect and good. This, of course, brings a new perspective to the idea of good and evil being two separate qualities in opposition to one another. Divine sparks override the idea of evil being separate; even so-called evil could not exist without being sustained by God. If this is so, we must conclude that there is a necessary place for some degree of "evil" in the divine cosmology.

Some say that free will could not operate if there were not an "apparent" choice between good and evil. The realization that God is everything does not preclude a universe that has a spiritual magnetism, with a pull toward the positive (good) pole and an opposing pull toward a negative (evil) pole. All can still be under one umbrella, often referred to as the wings of the Shekhina. "Good" and "evil" in this context suggest that the attraction of good pulls consciousness to increasingly higher levels of understanding, while the opposite attraction toward evil causes confusion and casts more and more veils over one's individual consciousness. Greater understanding leads to greater compassion and wisdom, while veiled consciousness results in increased ignorance, more mental suffering, and continued unskillful actions that can cause great pain in the world.

Obviously the angels we most wish to invoke and imagine are those that have "good" qualities of lovingkindness, strength, healing, the light of understanding, and so forth. But it is useful to know that there are also dark angels, the ones that pull us off track, that trip us, that confuse and seduce us with greed, lust, desire, and power.

Evil is introduced quite early in the Torah, immediately after the birthing of humans, in the second chapter of Genesis: "And God formed man ... and put man in the Garden ... and made in the middle of the Garden the Tree of Knowledge of Good and Evil" (Gen. 2:7–9). In the very next chapter, the serpent seduces the humans by saying, "God knows that the day you eat [the fruit of the Tree of Knowledge] … you will know good and evil, just like a god"(Gen. 3:4–5). A few chapters later, there were enough humans alive for God to regret the creation of humans. We find that "God saw that man's wickedness was so great that the human heart was continually thinking of evil" (Gen. 6:5), and so God decided to destroy this creation of humans. This is the beginning of the story of the Flood.

The sentence just prior to the one in which God sees the degree of man's wickedness, says that there were *nefilim* on earth in those days (Gen. 6:4). The standard translation for nefilim is giants, lizards, or other creatures who were the cause of the evil of those times. The root *n-f-l* means "to fall." It is from this that the idea of "fallen" angels is said to have been derived.

The initial reference to fallen angels in the Book of Enoch describes a group of two hundred guardian angels who descended on Mt. Hermon (in the north of present-day Israel) in the time of Jered, who was Enoch's father and Methuselah's grandfather. These guardian angels appeared as humans. There is a dispute about their intentions. One opinion says that their original purpose was to offer mankind the teachings of law and justice, but the daughters of men seduced these angels, and thus they fell. The other opinion is that their decision to descend was motivated by a lust they had already developed for the young girls. In either case, their "fall" was due to their consorting with human women.

The children born of these relationships were themselves giants who caused a great deal of destruction. At this time, men learned the use of weapons and other tools that caused much demonic destruction in contrast to the divine wisdom that was the natural state of the world. This was the beginning of human corruption, and it was this that led to the Flood.

There are other versions of how the fallen angels came to be, but almost everyone agrees that the leader of this group was and is Satan, also known as Belial or Samael. As Belial, Satan appears in the Dead Sea Scrolls as the head of the forces of darkness. As Samael, Satan is seen as the archangel Michael's primary foe. Initially, Satan appears in the Bible not as a proper noun, but as a common noun, "one who opposes," or as a verb meaning "to oppose or to obstruct." Later, in the books of prophets, Satan appears in proper-noun form as an individual who is the main prosecutor in the celestial courts. Satan becomes well established as the main adversarial character in the story of Job.

Satan plays both the role of tempter and accuser, often in the same story. When he succeeds as the tempter, even though he is the main cause of the ensuing confusion, the confusion becomes the issue used to prosecute the offender. Satan is viewed as the one primarily responsible for the major "sins" described in the Bible: the fall in the Garden, the golden calf, the story of Korach, the sin of David with Bathsheba, and others.

The point, of course, is that if we all lived exclusively with good angels, only under the influence of truth and clarity, we would have achieved the highest level of consciousness long ago. Yet the ever-unfolding universe is dependent upon a vast series of variables and unknowable factors that affect the shape of each moment. The tensions of opposing forces that have fairly equal strength are crucial in the give and take of how the universe manifests. If one side were to win dominance, the universe would accelerate in that direction; and without a counterforce, the universe would disappear. The essential structure of this universe is built upon polarities.

So part of life is to recognize those habitual forces that pull us deeper into confusion and ignorance, and to understand how to counter them. It is important to realize that the demonic forces are servants, not opponents, of Oneness. This means that we must respect that they are highly skilled in what they do—being tricky, devious, and persuasive. Each time we make a resolution, and then find ourselves breaking our resolve, we can recognize the power of these opponents. We need patience, wisdom, tenacity, self-discipline, self-compassion, and strong conviction to contend with these powers in a loving way, without rancor, anger, or hatred. Just as some angels can be destructive, avenging, and not-so-pleasant, so too can some "demons" be useful, kind, generous, and helpful.

You may have your own names for these tricksters. Some of the names that come up in the Western spiritual literature are *mazikim* (harmful spirits), *shaydim* (devils), *ruchot* (spirits), *kesilim* (spirits who fool, misguide, and poke fun), *lezim* (jesters who throw and move things like poltergeists), *shomer dafim* (guardians of holy books who injure those who leave books open, drop them, or who place them upside down on the shelf), *seirim* (hairy creatures who inhabit ruins), *maveytot* (demons associated with death), *deverim* (pestilence who accompanies YHVH on the warpath), *reshephim* (the plagues that follow after deverim), Aza'el (who lives in the wilderness, connected with Aza'zel, the scapegoat that gets thrown over a cliff onto rocks), *alukot* (vampires, leeches), *belial* (streams of destruction; no benefit; also "the spirit of perversion, the angel of darkness, the angel of destruction"), *masteymah* (enemy, opponent), *asmodeus* (evil demon, also a name of the king of demons), Beelzebub (sometime referred to as Lord of the Flies), and *ruach tezazit* (demon of madness).

This is a short list of hundreds of references that appear in the literature of demonology. The Talmud devotes a significant number of passages to caution readers on where demons lurk and how to avoid them. This subject is not treated lightly, and my personal experience is that one should be circumspect in playing with these energies. The more sensitive we are to the positive uses of invoking angelic energies, the more we must be attentive to the so-called dark forces. We must also keep in mind that these energies still bear the spark of the Divine, and we need not fear them. Simply know that there is much more happening in these spirit realms than we normally perceive or understand.

I am not offering techniques in this section for invoking this kind of energy. Rather, I am bringing your attention how to recognize them and how to realize their role in our thoughts and emotions. Every distracting or obscuring thought that arises in our minds can be viewed as a messenger of confusion. Every disturbing emotion is the same. When people begin to meditate, they quickly realize how little control they have over their own minds. The mind and feelings run here and there like a wild monkey swinging through branches at random, going nowhere.

We do not need to personify these dark or confusing energies, but it is important to know that they are not easily brought under control. We can, however, learn ways to calm our own thoughts, relax our own bodies, and balance our own emotions. There are many practices in many traditions that offer us basic instructions for finding peace of mind. Indeed, most spiritual paths ultimately have this as a primary goal.

In the end, we all discover that life is our main teacher. Daily life brings with it clarity and confusion, ease and difficulty, harmony and trouble; the list is endless. We do not have to characterize our experiences in terms of good and evil; we simply need to recognize what is happening, how it is unfolding, and how we are dealing with each situation, thought, or feeling that arises.

The greater our realization, the more we are able to understand the nature of things, the more we are able to bring a skillful response and reaction. So life constantly provides new challenges and new opportunities to make wise choices. Characterizing things in terms of good and evil, or angels and demons, simply gives us tools for recognition, and through this recognition we gain greater wisdom and compassion to each event that arises.

ANGEL OF DEATH

Death is arguably the greatest mystery in creation. Some subatomic particles have "life" spans of microseconds, and some trees live for thousands of years. Some stars exist for billions of years. And yet everything that exists will sooner or later cease to exist. When we fully realize this universal truth on a personal level, it can either liberate us or terrify us. Most people, however, do not ponder death until it enters our homes.

In the early days of spiritual inquiry, death was viewed as the enemy of life. Many stories were built upon cosmic battles between the two, and the natural assumption was that death was a force separate from the Godhead. As monotheism developed, however, there was no way to separate death from an all-powerful, all-knowing, ever-present God. So instead of being the great enemy of God, it was simply viewed as an aspect of creation—death as a natural law of the universe. While death represents the end of everyday consciousness, still it is not considered to be an evil opponent. Death is simply a messenger of God often referred to as the Angel of Death.

We might have thought that because death is inevitable, the Angel of Death is all-powerful and unstoppable. However, this is not a correct conclusion according to the oral tradition and the folklore of Judaism. Indeed, the Angel of Death is viewed in a wide variety of ways. It can be tricked, cajoled, turned back, debated, defeated, refused, deceived, and chased away. There are many ways to die. Moreover, dying out of this reality does not exclude other realities. Most important, it is taught that the way we "cross over" from one reality to another can bypass the Angel of Death altogether and occur as gently as a "kiss."

The Angel of Death sometimes appears as a brilliant flashing light accompanied by a sweet smell. Sometimes beautiful and glorious, at other times it has the appearance of a goat, ram, or ugly beast. It has been called the Prince of Darkness and at times has the name of Belial, an angel of hatred whose dominion is darkness. Death has a number of angel names. When death is related to wild animals, the name of death is *Meshabber* (angel of shattering). In relation to domestic animals death is called *Hemah* (angel of fever), and in relation to children, death is called *Mash'khit* (angel of slaughtering). Death also has the name of *Af* (angel of anger), and death over kings is known as *Kazfiel* (angel of destruction).

It is taught that death can be held off by the burning of certain incense, and that both Moses and his brother Aaron used this method. In fact, Aaron made the angel faint by holding a smoldering censer under it and then dragging it to the Tabernacle to lock it in! Moses chased death away three times and would only surrender himself to the Source, without an intermediary. The Angel of Death was stopped when other angels pleaded for Isaac's life. Abraham was able to hold off death in a struggle that cost some of his servants their lives; however, Abraham brought them back to life! Noah avoided death by hiding in the Ark.

The Talmudic sage Joshua ben Levi debated the Angel of Death and was able to steal its knife (without which Death was unable to do its "work"). At that moment, death was almost eliminated from the world. As the story goes, however, God demanded that ben Levi return Death's knife to its rightful owner; thus death continues to this day.

In the Jewish oral tradition, a mythical city called Luz is described, located at the place where Jacob set up a pillar named Beth-El, the house of God. As the story goes, the Angel of Death has no power in this city. The mystical teachings say that Luz is well hidden and can be approached only by a cave whose entrance can be found in the hollow of an almond tree. The inhabitants of the city of Luz never die while in the city. But it is also taught that they eventually grow weary of life and leave the city in order to die.

In addition, there is a mystical assertion that there is a little bone in every human body, called the luz, that can never be destroyed. All of these teachings suggest that every human has the potential beyond what we normally view as life, and there is a suggestion here that while our bodies may die, our souls may remain forever connected with the source of creation.

We learn from all of these stories that while death is inevitable, we have a range of ways in which we can choose to engage death. Much has to do with our level of consciousness and our ability to absorb the thoughts that arise as the various energies associated with death come up for us. Everyone, of course, must die in their own way. However, the practices described in this book on how to invoke angels can be extraordinarily beneficial in times of need for strength, healing, and blessing. In addition, these practices can be extremely useful in working with serious illness and with the dying process.

THE KISS OF THE SHEKHINA

It is taught that the Divine Presence will often gently take a person's life rather than giving that soul over to the Angel of Death. The metaphor for this way of dying is described as the "kiss of the Shekhina." Many have been taken in this way.

One of the sweetest and most important teachings of the Zohar centers on this idea of gentle dying. It describes in a number of sections this kind of dying as the most profound love that can be experienced. One section begins with a zoharic sage, Rabbi Isaac, offering a quote from the Song of Songs: "... kiss me with the kisses of the mouth" (Song of Songs 1:2). Rabbi Isaac explains: "... kissing expresses the cleaving of spirit to spirit. Therefore, one who dies by the kiss of God is united with a unique spirit [of love], a spirit which can never be separated from God (Zohar II:124b).

In a different section, the Zohar asks, "What prompted King Solomon, when recording words of love between the upper and the lower worlds, to begin with the words [in the Song of Songs], 'Let him kiss me'? The reason is that no other love is as ecstatic as the moment when spirit cleaves to spirit—breath to breath—in a kiss. When mouth meets mouth, spirits unite and become one single love" (Zohar II:146b).

In the same section the Zohar also teaches

> ... the kiss of love expands in four directions and these are uni-
> fied in one word: *ahavah*, meaning "love," which is a holy chariot [a
> vehicle to higher consciousness]. These four letters [*a-h-v-a*] are the
> four directions of the love and joy of the [four] limbs. When love
> develops in a breath-to-breath kiss, it ascends and meets with a chief
> angel [Sandalphon] who is so large, it towers over one thousand
> nine hundred and ninety firmaments. Nonetheless, despite its size
> and magnitude, if Sandalphon attempts to prevent the spirit from
> proceeding, it will not succeed. Sandalphon cannot stop love, and

love will make its way to the Palace of Love—the source of all love. Concerning this matter, Solomon teaches, "Many waters cannot quench love, neither can the floods drown it" (Song of Songs 8:7).

The Zohar continues: "When that love-spirit enters the Palace of Love, the yearning for the supernal kisses is aroused so that the kisses of the supernal love are duly brought forth, and they are the beginning of the awakening of all supernal love, attachment and union." For this reason the Song of Songs begins with the words: "Let It kiss me ..." Who is "It"? "It" is a secret that is hidden within the supernal concealment.

Understand this! The Most Hidden Secret is unknowable, however it can be revealed as an ephemeral brightness that shines on a narrow path that illuminates and penetrates everything. This is the starting point of all mysteries. Still it is at times discoverable [for those who know the secret teachings of how to open themselves], but even for those who are not able to realize this brightness, still, kissing mouth-to-mouth leads to love and love ascends to merge at its source in the Palace of Love. So, even though the Most Hidden Secret is beyond the comprehension of most humans, the Song of Songs gives us a hint in the profound hidden teaching in the words, "Let It kiss me ..." (Zohar II:146b).

Thus the Kabbalah teaches that somewhere deep within, each of us can be kissed by the Divine Spirit, and this kiss will forever bind us to our essential nature. We all want to be kissed by a beloved so that the beloved merges within us for eternity, both in this world and in other realms. While we may not be touched in this way during our lives, we still have an opportunity to merge with the Divine up to our last breath. In this extraordinary teaching, we learn that we can "go over" in a way as if being "kissed" by God, which assures an eternal love.

As we come to a close on these mystical teachings, I feel drawn to tell the story of my father's death. It had and continues to have a profound effect on me. Dad was mostly unhappy after retirement and became increasingly miserable and sad as he grew more physically incapacitated. In his early eighties, he became more and more dependent upon a wheelchair. In his own home, his bed was moved down to the den, as he could no longer climb the stairs. He began to refer to this room as his jail cell. From that time forward, every room he lived in was perceived as a cell. After Mom died, he declined into a slow, creeping dementia.

In his late eighties, he spoke about not wanting to go on. Despite these words, he had a strong will to live. In many ways, life was a torment, but the will to continue kept him going into his early nineties. At that point he was completely alienated from the world—angry, lonely, and without much memory. He could not recall my name but knew that I was a figure of authority and therefore the enemy. He would not let me stay long in his room and chased me out by yelling or ignoring me altogether.

When his time came to die, we were called by the nursing home. My wife, Shoshana, and I rushed to his room. He was in considerable pain. He allowed the nursing aides to touch him but pushed me away. As the illness took him closer to the edge, however, something softened inside of him, and he started to release into a new mind state. He began to gaze at something I could not see, a gaze that indicated he was being touched somewhere deep and intimate. I believe it was "that place" where we all want to be touched.

At that point, something pulled me to reach out yet once more. This time he reached back and took my hand. Once connected, I could feel the presence of something profound, something so welcoming I wanted only to be held by it. My dad now squeezed my hand, and I was in his field in a strange way such that I was seeing through his own inner eye. I found myself repeating words of reassurance—"It's okay, it's okay"—both for him and for me, over and over again.

Mom, having died nine years earlier, was there with us. It was she who led his soul out of his dying body. And it was indeed like a kiss, but so much more than lips meeting. It was just as they say—breath within breath, two breaths becoming one. At the last moment, after the final breath, he shed one tear—and, despite all our difficulties over the years, my heart opened to him forever.

The experience of this kind of love is simply to learn how to surrender to each moment as it arises, to let go in the arms of the Divine, to yield—not attempting to control anything—and to discover the true faith that arises. We are always and forever connected by our breath to the source of breath, and we always have access to the Palace of Love, which is our certain destiny—all we need do is realize it and relax into the everlasting arms of the Divine.

Finally, please again play Track 7: Meditation on the Shekhina. Once again let yourself melt and merge into the delightful experience of resting in the arms of the Divine. When we are able to do so, we realize in the depths of our beings

LISTEN TO TRACK 7
Meditation on the Shekhina

that we are not alone. Indeed, we are never alone. We are immersed in a multitude of realities. Everything that happens, everything we see or touch, is all an expression of the Divine. Knowing this opens our hearts, softens our minds, and brings a light of awareness and clarity that forever changes our lives. ❖

Acknowledgments

THERE IS A Hasidic teaching that before we are born, our souls gather with many other souls to make agreements on how we will interact when we are born in our new bodies on earth. Our souls meet the souls of our parents-to-be, siblings, teachers, partners, acquaintances, friends, and most certainly our lovers. All of these relationships throughout our lives unfold in ways that cause the souls to influence one another along the lines of our previous agreements, gently or harshly, lovingly or angrily, smoothly or roughly, always in ways that affect us deeply. And each time one soul interacts with another soul, it is the same as one angel connecting with another.

I have had the good fortune to have been able to recognize many of these angels in my life for what they have given me. At the top of my list is my wife of almost three decades, Shoshana, who every day over these years as partner, best friend, and lover, has contributed her own angel dust, smoothing out rough edges and bringing clarity—at times with subtlety, at others with tough love. It is a great blessing to communicate well and to be compelled to face the truth about ourselves, however challenging that may be.

Of course, major angels in my life were the members of my immediate family, Sam and Helene, my father and mother, may they rest in peace; and Ralph and Mark, my two brothers, may they live long and healthy lives.

Also very high on my most-important angel list as a friend and loyal, steadfast supporter for close to twenty years is Alan Secrest, who now owns the business of Cooper-Secrest Associates.

Many spiritual teachers have been angels for me, most prominently Rabbi Zalman Schachter-Shalomi, who taught me the difference between what it means to be a rabbi versus a rebbe—a rabbi being a teacher and a rebbe being someone who is in special communion with a higher source. Reb Zalman, as my rebbe, was willing to ordain me as a rabbi. Another influential rebbe was R. Shlomo Carlebach, who gave the world thousands of amazing melodies.

Other major teaching angels have been Pir Vilayat Khan, who initiated me (and Shoshana) into the Sufi Order of the West; Zen master Bernie Glassman, who taught me about homelessness on the Bowery of New York City as well as about life—and mostly death—at Auschwitz. In addition, key teachers in my life have been some from other realms: Krishnamurti, Ramana Maharshi, and Shivapuri Baba, as well as a number who are alive and well, thank goodness: Joseph Goldstein, Sharon Salzberg, Jack Kornfield, Tsoknyi Rinpoche, Eckhart Tolle, and Adyashanti—all great teachers.

I could easily add a hundred names to this list. Those of us who are spiritual seekers in this day and age are blessed to have easy access to so many incredible teachings, more than at any time in the history of human consciousness.

Some publishers have been outstanding resources. In the audio field, a major angel for tens of thousands of people is Tami Simon, founder of Sounds True, who makes available to the world a vast array of wisdom teachings. I must give special thanks as well to Mitchell Clute and Kelly Notaras of Sounds True, who worked diligently to make this a useful book and CD.

Among my greatest angels are people who are students and friends who have shared ideas, questions, thoughts, and observations on the various practices we have done together on challenging meditation retreats. Something happens to us in silent practice that occasionally pulls us back to that time before our birth when our souls made commitments to one another. The soul and angel worlds become quite "real" when sitting in silence for long hours.

I have deep gratitude for all who have touched my life, all you fabulous angels. And to you who read these words, I thank you for taking the time. May you be blessed to be able to recognize more about the angels in your own life, for it is certain that by doing so your heart will open and soften— and the guardian angel living within you will be able to touch others in its own way that will, I hope, help to raise consciousness to bring this world ever closer to a lasting peace and harmony. ❖

About the Author

RABBI DAVID A. COOPER has been called "one of today's leading teachers of Jewish meditation." He is an active student of the world's great spiritual traditions and is the author of many books, including *Three Gates to Meditation Practice* (Skylight), *A Heart of Stillness* (Skylight), *A Handbook of Jewish Meditation* (Jewish Lights), and *Ecstatic Kabbalah* (Sounds True). His book *God Is a Verb: Kabbalah and the Practice of Mystical Judaism* (Riverhead/Putnam) has been highly acclaimed and was nominated for the National Jewish Book Award. It has sold over 100,000 copies and has been translated into several languages.

Cooper and his wife, Shoshana, lead Jewish meditation retreats nationwide throughout the year. Rabbi Cooper can be engaged to teach weekend intensives and retreats in meditation and Kabbalah. His Web site is www.rabbidavidcooper.com, and he can be reached at davidcoop99@yahoo.com.

SOUNDS TRUE was founded with a clear vision: to disseminate spiritual wisdom. Located in Boulder, Colorado, Sounds True publishes teaching programs that are designed to educate, uplift, and inspire. With more than 550 titles available, we work with many of the leading spiritual teachers, thinkers, healers, and visionary artists of our time.

For a free catalog please contact Sounds True via the World Wide Web at www.soundstrue.com, call us toll free at 800-333-9185, or write: The Sounds True Catalog, PO Box 8010, Boulder CO 80306.

SOUNDS TRUE
awakening wisdom

CD SESSIONS

1. *Archangel Meditation (short form)* 10:02

2. *Wise Guide Meditation* 5:36

3. *Guardian Angel Meditation* 9:49

4. *Archangel Meditation (long form)* 13:53

5. *Meditation on Metatron* 7:09

6. *Meditation on Sandalphon* 5:43

7. *Meditation on the Shekhina* 11:46

Total Running Time 64:03